Justice for Gays and Lesbians

To order additional copies, please contact us.
BookSurge, LLC
www.booksurge.com
1-866-308-6235
orders@booksurge.com

Justice for Gays and Lesbians

Reclaiming Christian Fundamentals
Crisis and Challenge in the Episcopal Church

Robert L. McCan, PhD.

2006

Justice for Gays and Lesbians

TABLE OF CONTENTS

ACKNOWLEDGEMENTS

I entered a flowing river of support when I began to write this book. Research materials I needed became readily available. I was serving as a group leader in a church program titled Disciples of Christ in Community (DOCC). At the course conclusion an unofficial support group formed that did research, typed, and reviewed early drafts of the manuscript—and prayed.

Early in the process my rector, the Rev. Pierce Klemmt, offered me three bulging manila folders containing articles, book reviews, addresses and Bible studies he had read and filed for over 25 years—all under the title, "homosexuality." He encouraged me to climb into the boat and go on the journey downstream.

Four persons made special contributions to the finished manuscript. The early editor was Sidney "Pepper" Smith, a young man I met in DOCC. I learned that he went to journalism school and taught creative writing at a college. After a stint in the Peace Corps in China he came to Washington, D.C. in the hope of pursuing a career as a poet. I liked his poems and wanted to include one by him, if he chose to write one for the book. He did.

The second person, Betty K. Hart, did heavy rowing in this flowing stream. She and Frank, her husband, sit a pew ahead of us each Sunday in church. We began casual conversations after services. I learned that she is active in our diocese and in the national Church. In fact, she was present during the entire debate in Minneapolis when the Church made its historic decision.

Betty has worked tirelessly to clarify the workings of General Convention, to provide perspective on women's issues, and in general to help proofread the text and make sure the facts are correct. Betty is an historian, a life-long advocate for justice, and a person who loves the Episcopal Church. The book is markedly better because of her help.

Near the end of this process my daughter, Susanna MacGregor, took time from her job in Iowa do final editing and to put the manuscript into the form required for publication. Father and daughter had a wonderful time working together on the project and learning from each other. Her Harvard education served us well.

My wife, Peggy, read the manuscript one more time. Her love of language composition and her expertise with crossword puzzles helped clear the brush from the stream and her suggestions helped avoid rocky shoals.

Finally, my stepson, Jason Fleming, designed the cover. As a child he attended art school at the Corcoran Art Gallery in Washington, D.C. His early career was in music and graphic design. I gave him a general idea of what I wanted to achieve on the cover and he produced it. He is a truly creative person.

To these persons and a host of others unnamed who have contributed directly to this book, I say a heartfelt "thank you." In the end, my decisions based on my scholarship and my anger at injustice are expressed in these pages.

Introduction
THIS I BELIEVE

> John to the seven churches that are in Asia: Grace to
> you and peace from him who is and who was and who
> is to come....
> —St. John the Divine, Revelation 1:4

John, the author of Revelation, wrote to seven specific
churches. But seven was also a symbolic number signifying that
the message was for the larger world. In that sense, I write this
book to churches of all denominations and even to our secular
society, although I focus specifically on the experience of the
Episcopal Church of the United States. I am most mindful of
our common search for understanding as we together confront
the important and divisive issue of homosexuality.

With the Episcopal Church I make the case for inclusion;
for other denominations the book can be read as a case study
of the fundamental issues that led to the ordination of the
Episcopal Church's first openly gay bishop.

I write to denominational leaders, to beleaguered bishops,
to struggling clergy and to a divided laity. I write as a biblical
interpreter, theologian and an ethicist. I write as a minister
of fifteen years in Baptist churches but also as one who came
from an interdenominational seminary, with a doctorate from
one affiliated with the Church of Scotland. For many years I
was accused of being a Baptist with a Presbyterian accent. For
a time I held a high level academic post as Special Assistant to
the Director of the Woodrow Wilson International Center for
Scholars in the Smithsonian Institution. Later I taught political

ethics at a United Methodist Seminary, while at the same time I was a senior staff member at The Churches' Center for Theology and Public Policy, a think-tank supported by most mainline Protestant denominations and the Roman Catholic Church. My point of reference is the Episcopal Church, where I have worshipped and sometimes witnessed as a member for the past twenty-five years.

This book is an unapologetic endorsement of and rationale for my Church's position on homosexuality. I approach the issue from many perspectives. First, I review the "forty years in the wilderness" as Episcopalians struggled with adopting a policy of inclusion. I then highlight the same struggle being played out on the stage of mainline Protestant churches. Then I present an overview of homosexuality and provide an analysis of why the Episcopal Church made its historic shift. But I go deeper. The issue of homosexuality cannot be considered adequately without revisiting the fundamental claims of the Christian faith.

I address pastors of congregations with gay and lesbian members. It is hard for ministers to give emotional support and spiritual strength if the denomination condemns homosexuality as incompatible with Christian teaching. I offer practical ways to help congregations deal with their homophobia.

I then change the focus to the bedrock biblical call for justice and show how gays and lesbians face unfair and even deadly discrimination.

Of course, Christians want to know what the Bible has to say. I examine every passage of scripture that makes reference to homosexuality. My conclusions are new to many but familiar to those in the Episcopal Church who have studied the issue. I have drawn on the scholarship of others and from official studies commissioned by the Episcopal Church and other denominations. A less conventional analysis is found in my presentation of the life and teachings of Jesus. I show the way he used Hebrew law and the wisdom literature to interpret that law as a new ethic of love. I also show how Jesus used scripture, and how he rejected all claims of inerrancy for the Hebrew Bible.

While our ethic is based on the fundamental principle of love for God and for neighbor, we need more practical guidance on how to make moral decisions. So there is a chapter on the basic questions of ethics: the right, the good, and the prudent. I show how the Responsible Self takes into account eternal moral principles, the greatest good in a specific circumstance, and what is prudent to reach ethical conclusions. I then turn to inquire into the creative nature of the One who is constantly doing new things for humanity.

After reaching a clear perspective on the teachings of Jesus, the nature of Christian ethical decisions, and the loving, creative nature of God, I want to listen and learn from homosexual persons I have known, and from writings of gays and lesbians giving their perspectives. I find that some among us stereotype and condemn without hearing the other side of the debate. I see first hand and read daily in the newspapers of the human wreckage we cause gay and lesbian persons by not accepting them as they are. I then consider in more detail the issue of same-gender marriage, where I make the case that this development is Christian and humane for the lesbian and gay persons involved. Further, doing the spiritual work necessary to reach this level of inclusiveness is also a means of salvation for the Church.

As I approach the end of the book, I write to the worldwide Anglican Communion, comprised of seventy-eight million members, the largest sector and the fastest growing being the Anglican Church in Africa. This world body disagreed with the decision of the Episcopal Church of the United States to elect and consecrate a bishop who was divorced and then living in an open committed union with another man. The larger Anglican Communion asked the American Church to explain more fully its actions biblically, ethically and theologically, so they could better understand the reasons behind the decisions that were made. This entire book could be read as a general response to the Anglican Communion, and one chapter addresses it specifically.

Finally, I place this contentious issue in a larger context as I evaluate what is happening to Christianity in this country and around the world. I look beyond Christianity to discover the same tensions in each of the major world religions. On one side are those in each religion who fear loss of identity and purpose by reaching out to others and so they pull back into fundamentalism. On the other side are those who adapt to a global community with its diversity, yet seek a stable rudder in their ancient faiths. I suggest that the road taken by the Episcopal Church in regard to homosexuality is a moderate and rational way forward in building our future as Christian churches and as members of the world community. I suggest that we may be participants in God's grand design for the world's future.

I do the hard work of Bible study, ethics, and theology because this issue does not stand alone. Unless devout Christians can see acceptance of homosexuality as consistent with the scripture, the love ethic of Jesus, the nature of God, and Christian ethical living, they will not take this vital step. I make the case that we are reclaiming Christian fundamentals. We are following our Master in the most profound way by welcoming homosexual persons.

When we confront the fact of homosexuality in church

or society, we generate strong emotions. I took on this project because I felt it needed doing. I am aware that I may provoke negative reactions in some circles; for some I may become a public enemy. My goal is to follow the example of Jesus to the best of my ability, speaking up against injustice and those who keep people from God, while forgiving any animosity that may be directed toward me personally.

I write as a Christian, primarily to other believers. I recognize that there is a cultural divide between the church and secular society. I know that many outside the church are interested in what I am saying but dislike working their way through the church jargon and ecclesiastical issues. I know there are many gay and lesbian persons who are vitally interested in this topic, though many have long since given up on the church. I invite those in the secular community to stay with me and, at the end of the day, consider again the prospect of aligning with the church, which remains as the legacy of Jesus in the modern world.

While the church is undoubtedly on the wrong side of history on many issues, this book shows how reform movements have most often come from those touched by the spirit of Jesus as found in the New Testament. The real gospel is an exciting invitation and a great challenge. I also urge those in other denominations to work from within their church structures to fling open the doors and welcome all persons to the great banquet feast. For those in denominations where the doors are locked and the keys appear to be lost, I invite you to a banquet seat in the Episcopal Church or another whose welcoming doors are open.

I am bold in speaking truth to power. I sharply disagree with the Roman Catholic Church on sexuality. Such criticism pains me deeply because I have such great respect for the mother

Church, especially for profound social teachings on justice and concern for the poor. I also criticize the traditionalists within our denomination and the fundamentalist Christian movement that in many ways is only superficially biblical and is often aligned with injustice. Some evangelicals are aligned with the love ethic of Jesus, but as a whole Christian fundamentalism veers far to the right and is now part of the problem rather than the solution. That movement to the right forced my departure from the Southern Baptist Convention.

Finally, I speak truth to power in the Anglican Communion in ways that I prefer to avoid. I have spent parts of several years working in Africa for the U.S. Agency for International Development, and have been a Board Member of an Episcopal foundation working in several countries in Africa. I love Africa, and I have been honored to know bishops and other church leaders in Africa who have witnessed with great courage and have evangelized with great joy. Nonetheless, I gently but firmly speak words of rebuke in the spirit of love.

We turn now to the intense forty year struggle within the Episcopal Church that moved us gradually from a traditional position that rejected homosexuality to a new inclusiveness.

Chapter 1
WRESTLING WITH GOD

> Jacob was left alone; and a man wrestled with
> him until daybreak.... Then the man said, "You
> shall no longer be called Jacob, but Israel, for
> you have striven with God and with humans
> and have prevailed."
> —Genesis 32: 24, 26

If ever there was protracted wrestling with God,
it is occurring in mainline Protestant churches as we
seek the peace and blessing of God in deciding about
homosexuality in our common life. Jacob's all-night
encounter left him lame, as a lasting reminder of this
pivotal struggle. It changed his life and even his name.
The churches cannot expect to reach daybreak unscathed.
We can have faith that justice will prevail as we strive
with God and with humans. Further, we can hope to gain
a more profound understanding of our own identity from
the experience.

The primary focus of this study is the Episcopal
Church because, for this denomination, daybreak
has come and the decisive struggle has ended with
the Church's decision to include gays and lesbians
as candidates for holy orders. It is also the author's
denomination, giving him more detailed experience of
the depths and heights of reflection and action there.
This wrestling with God is requiring tremendous energy
as each denomination pleads with the Almighty for

1

relief, blessing and wholeness. In this chapter we look first at the protracted struggle of the Episcopal Church. We then enter the agony and joy of six other mainline denominations that are confronted with the same issues. We note that the cause of mainline church splintering at the time of Civil War was the Abolitionist movement. The Episcopal and the Congregationalist churches best weathered that controversy, and they have done so again in this latest dispute.

Dr. Martin Marty observed the furor in each denomination over acceptance of homosexual persons and used a well-worn sermon illustration from the nineteenth century to indicate what he saw happening. In a quiet town a church building caught on fire. Everyone was surprised to see the village atheist at the head of the bucket brigade. Someone asked him, "Why are you showing up now?" He responded while pouring a bucket of water on the flames, "Because when the church is on fire is the only time that anything exciting is going on."

Our teachable moment comes when the church is on fire and we have to respond. It seems to take a crisis to get us to do new thinking on an old position. When Martin Luther King Jr. went to Birmingham jail he was confronted by distinguished clergy, black and white, who wrote an open letter to him, published in the city newspaper. The clergy suggested that he stop agitating for a time and let the tensions cool. They felt he was not helping his cause or theirs by pushing so hard. His response was "A Letter from Birmingham Jail." He used soaring language and powerful prose to make his arguments on why he should press on, with references to scripture, history, and philosophy. The country was ready for the first time to pass the Voting Rights Act after black and white met fierce resistance as they marched together from Birmingham to Selma. He could have accepted the advice to go slow, in which case we might still be going through this trauma. If so, African-Americans might have endured another 40 years without the right to vote.

Our crisis is a crossroad. Are we a fire-fighting brigade trying to dampen the flames of injustice or do we wait and watch as the fire burns? Will we use this difficult time to forge a more just position on a highly volatile issue that the world will no longer let us ignore? Our crisis is also our time of opportunity.

EPISCOPAL CHURCH USA

This section recounts highlights of the struggle in the Episcopal Church in dealing with homosexuality. From one perspective this has been a wonderful example of Christians reasoning together. It is the Anglican Way of listening and praying together. The Church could move forward only by achieving a consensus. Churches that issue edicts are not subject to this arduous process; neither do they get to participate in a process of learning and spiritual growth. But before moving into the crisis and challenge surrounding homosexuality it may be instructive to understand briefly the history and structure of this branch of Christendom.

The Protestant Episcopal Church in the United States is part of the worldwide Anglican Communion. It is independent, yet works cooperatively within the 78,000,000 member body of Anglicans. There are approximately 2,500,000 members in some 7,000 parishes and missions, with about 14,000 clergy. There are 106 dioceses and mission districts. The governing body of the Church is General Convention, which meets every three years for an extended nine to ten day time of prayer, deliberation and decision-making. Each Diocese has a Diocesan Bishop elected by clergy and laity and confirmed by the national church. General Convention is comprised of a House of Bishops and a House of Deputies, the latter being composed of an equal number of clergy and lay persons. According to the constitution, in any matter of disagreement between the two houses, the deputies outrank the bishops. (Additional information on the history of the Episcopal Church and its relationship to the Worldwide Anglican Communion is found in the Appendix at the end of the book.)

On issues related to homosexuality the balance of opinion in the Episcopal Church shifted over 40 years to the "tipping point" when the Church accepted the decision made by the diocese of New Hampshire to consecrate the Rev. Canon V. Gene Robinson as Bishop. While the issue was pushed to the forefront by the necessity of making a decision about this election and consecration, the preponderance of opinion had been moving in that direction at a slow and laborious pace, always marked by dispute, agony and study. In some respects the Episcopal Church was like the children of Israel wandering in the wilderness for 40 years before crossing over into a promised land.

The saga begins modestly in 1964 when the 61st General Convention emphasized a study of human sexuality. A report from the Standing Commission on the Church in Human Affairs noted the turbulence in society around the breakdown of family life and the meaning of

human sexuality. It concluded that the Church, mindful
of its responsibility to give leadership in all areas of
human conduct, instructed the Executive Council
to gather data, formulate studies, and make specific
recommendations to the 1967 General Convention. Such
studies were in place at the 62nd General Convention,
where the term "homosexuality" was used for the first
time.

At the 65th General Convention in 1976 the debate
was joined when deputies accepted homosexual persons
as children of God. A resolution was adopted that said
in part, "homosexual persons are children of God who
have a full and equal claim with all other persons upon
the love, acceptance and pastoral concern and care of the
Church." Another resolution recognized the "substantial
contributions" gay and lesbian members were making to
the life of the Church and society. The first resolution
created considerable consternation after some proponents
expressed their belief that the word "acceptance" implied
the right for same-gender blessing as a symbolic form of
marriage.

This issue moved to the center in January of 1977
when Bishop Paul Moore of New York, with the consent
of the Standing Committee, ordained as a deacon a self-
declared homosexual, Ellen Marie Barrett. Bishop Moore
praised her "courage" in identifying with the lesbian
community and said Jesus himself included everyone
except the self-righteous Pharisees.

The House of Bishops convened in October of that
year in Port St. Lucie, Florida and received a report
from the Commission on Theology, which stated, "The
Church is right to confine its nuptial blessings exclusively

to heterosexual marriage. Homosexual unions witness to incompleteness." In another section that dealt with ordination, the Bishops' report stated, "In the case of an advocating and/or practicing homosexual" ordination is inadmissible because "it involves the Church in a public denial of its own theological and moral norms." Many hoped that Bishop Moore was properly chastised.

The Church appeared to be speaking from two positions at the same time. The 66th General Convention in 1979 affirmed a new position in a resolution on ordination that stated there should not be a barrier to ordination of any qualified person, either heterosexual or homosexual. But another statement went to the heart of the matter, "The traditional teachings of the Church on marriage, marital fidelity, and sexual chastity remain in effect. Candidates for ordination are expected to conform to this standard.... It is not appropriate for this Church to ordain a practicing homosexual."

Differing positions, however, did not disappear. Twenty members of the House of Bishops proceeded to sign a minority report. They affirmed the "ministries of ordained persons known to be homosexual...." They went on to declare, "Not all of these persons have been celibate; and in the relationships of many of them, maintained in the face of social hostility and against great odds, we have seen a redeeming quality which in its way and according to its mode is no less a sign to the world of God's love than is the more usual sign of Christian marriage."

The positions changed little until at the 69th Convention in 1988, the Standing Commission on Human Affairs and Health reported significant changes in society as a reason to review sexual standards. It noted that a majority in the Church wanted to reaffirm traditional moral standards, but a minority "of this Church is convinced that the time has come to begin a process that will enable Christians to think through new moral and sexual options in the light of new realities."

The report did not recommend any legislation, but rather asked for a greater measure of openness and understanding. The Commission urged the Church to create a setting in which homosexual persons could tell their stories and be heard with respect.

In response to the Commission, fifty-two conservative bishops then asked that a statement from the 1987 Synod of the Church of England be included in the Convention Journal. That statement expressed the view that homosexual acts fall short of the Christian ideal and the response of the homosexual person must be repentance.

In 1989 the Rt. Rev. John S. Spong, with the consent of the Standing Committee of the Diocese of Newark and after written notification to the Presiding Bishop and the House of Bishops, ordained the Rev. Robert Williams, "a homosexual person living in a public, avowed relationship with a person of the same sex." Bishop Spong based his action on his belief that the 1979 resolution was commended to the Church but was not a legislative requirement. Following this "first" ordination of an openly practicing homosexual priest, the House of Bishops, meeting in Washington, D.C. in September of 1990 reaffirmed the 1979 resolution of General Convention stating that the ordination of "a practicing homosexual or any person who is engaged in heterosexual relations outside of marriage" is inappropriate. The

House of Bishops stated their belief that Bishop Spong had acted without proper authority, but they recognized that support for his position was growing. They counseled tolerance and healing to promote reconciliation.

Two more highly publicized ordinations followed in quick succession, one in Newark and the other in the Diocese of Washington. Still other ordinations of openly homosexual persons occurred without being widely publicized. It was in this highly charged atmosphere that the 70th General Convention met in Phoenix in 1991. In preparation, the Standing Commission on Human Affairs had asked all dioceses to discuss homosexuality and try to gain understanding and consensus. The Commission reported that only 28 of 99 dioceses had submitted reports on dialogues they were to have held and noted that fewer than half of the dioceses had complied with the request to have these discussions. Finally the Commission concluded that no consensus had been achieved.

The Standing Commission on Human Affairs of this Convention then issued its own statement, which included a defense of homosexuality. It noted that sexuality is often misused and stated that any exploitative sexual practice should be condemned. It went on to state that homosexual orientation is not inconsistent with being a Christian and opposed the argument that homosexual persons need to attempt a transformation into heterosexuality. The report made the case that human beings are not meant to be alone and that committed same-gender relationships are to be commended. It argued that homophobia is rampant both in society and within the Church and should be rooted out. Finally, the Commission recommended that liturgical forms be developed for use in blessing gay and lesbian same-gender covenants.

This 70th General Convention as a whole then reaffirmed its traditional positions, while in practice it moved toward acceptance of homosexual ordination and the blessing of same-gender couples. The Convention authorized the House of Bishops to prepare a Pastoral Study Document to promote further dialogue and asked that it be completed before the 71st Convention. In urging dioceses and local parishes to spend time in prayerful study and discussion, the House of Bishops noted that "our greatest resource is the communion we have with each other, sustained by the Holy Spirit."

After doing a biblical analysis of marriage and teachings on homosexuality, the study guide, issued on behalf of the bishops, turned to a sociological study of human sexuality and the experiences of gay and lesbian persons. It cited several research studies indicating that homosexual persons believe their condition is something they inherit and is not a choice. They discussed the trauma endured by most adolescents who are gay and lesbian and noted that teenage suicide is two to three times as prevalent among this youth population. The study completed this section with the conclusion, "Clergy and church friends can play an important role in creating a safe environment and in supporting gay/lesbian parishioners...."

The study document was offered to the Church as an opportunity for further evaluation. Yet, it noted, "The teaching of the church holds that the normative context of sexual intimacy is lifelong heterosexual monogamous marriage."

Discussion and maneuver continued during the next three conventions. Reports from Committees recognized the strong divergence of views. In each case the formal conclusion was for the Church to stand on its traditional consensus. Yet, the minority position was growing. More deputies were voting for acceptance. There seemed also to be more openness among deputies to the possibility that acceptance of homosexuality was closer to the mind of Christ than the old position. While the large majority of communicants in the pews were hardly aware of the political and theological battles that were raging, the move toward acceptance now seemed to keen observers to be just a matter of time.

Perhaps the most significant event during these years was a trial in 1995, which in retrospect may have foreshadowed the tipping point in favor of accepting homosexual persons. On January 27, 1995, ten bishops filed a presentment against Bishop Walter Righter, a retired bishop who had accepted a new position as assistant bishop in the Diocese of Newark. In 1990 he had ordained to the diaconate an openly partnered homosexual.

There were two charges: (1) He taught publicly that a practicing homosexual may properly be ordained, and (2) he ordained a practicing homosexual, in violation of his ordination vows to conform to the core doctrines of the Church. A sufficient number of bishops voted favorably on the presentment to require a church trial, held in May of 1996.

The ecclesiastical court found in favor of Bishop Walter Righter. The Judge, the Presenters and the Respondent had all agreed that the key issue was to determine what constituted "core doctrine." The Judge decided that core doctrine describes the essence of Christianity contained in the early creeds. The Court concluded, "...there is no Core Doctrine prohibiting the ordination of a non-celibate homosexual person living in a faithful and committed sexual relationship with a person of the same sex...."

The 72nd General Convention in 1997 passed a resolution offering hope to those seeking a change in official policy, and pointed the way toward the action taken in 2003. The resolution apologized on behalf of the Episcopal Church to its members who are gay and lesbian as well as to lesbians and gays outside the Church for the years of rejection and maltreatment by the Church. It asked the Church to repent of its sins committed against lesbian and gay people—physical, psychological and spiritual—through covert and overt action and inaction. Episcopalians, it said, seek amendment of life and ask for God's help in sharing the Good News to all people.

The possible election and consecration of the Rev. V. Gene Robinson as Bishop of New Hampshire overshadowed all other reports, plans and activities at the 74th General Convention in Minneapolis in 2003. The Bishops met separately in debate and prayer. The entire body of deputies met together and heard arguments on all sides. Background papers were prepared and distributed by advocates of each position. Those who were present as observers at the time of the vote noted that there was a hushed presence of the Holy Spirit as deputies prayed, reflected on the biblical, theological and ethical issues and on the politics of a potential split in the Church. With full awareness of all of these factors and with all deliberateness, at the end of the day the vote was taken, reported in silence, and the session concluded with the Chaplain's prayer. Some two-thirds of deputies and bishops had voted affirmatively. The Church declared a new chapter in its ministry and witness.

After taking the huge step of supporting the election of Bishop Robinson, General Convention preferred to step back and take a deep breath. Bishop Peter James Lee of Virginia asked the Standing Committee on Liturgy and Music to delete their proposal to develop rites of blessing for same-gender relationships. His request was accepted. Bishop Lee wrote on August 3, 2003: "The Church is not of one mind on the issue of same-sex partnerships. Earlier this year the Primates of the churches of the Worldwide Anglican Communion discouraged the member churches of the Communion from developing rites of blessing for such relationships. In respect for the unity of our Communion, I will oppose proposals for same-sex blessings that come before this convention."

As the Convention drew to a close, voting participants and associated church groups, including Episcopal Church Women, gathered a final time on Friday, August 8 to share a liturgy and hear a sermon from the Presiding Bishop, The Most Reverend Frank T. Griswold. The Church's spiritual leader expressed pride in the civility of the discussion and noted how stories in the press expressed their admiration. "I think, however, that our civility is not the point. It is not civility that is working among us, but love. To be sure, there has been a certain amount of sinfulness on all sides, but there has also been a tremendous amount of grace at work as well.

It is love that gives us that desire to enter into the pain of the other and to bear it as one's own."

In a post-convention **Letter to the Church** dated August 20, 2003, Presiding Bishop Griswold reiterated his gratitude for the sensitivity and mutual respect that characterized the debate. Perhaps as much in hope of God's grace as from hard evidence, he concluded the letter, "We are members one of another, differentiated and yet one, not according to our notion of unity but one in the power of the Holy Spirit who binds us together."

Christ Church, Alexandria, Virginia, home of the writer, followed the pattern of most parishes across the country after General Convention. The Rector, the Rev. Pierce Klemmt, preached two sermons devoted to the debate and vote on Bishop Robinson's acceptance and then arranged parish discussions so that members could ask questions, listen and learn, and, yes, vent their frustration and anger at "what is happening to destroy our church." In a discussion session chaired by the Rector, members raised a number of questions and issues including the following:

- You have said the church has been at a crossroads like this before. Could you give me an example of what you have in mind? Lest you respond in the same way as others to whom I have put the question, and cite the ordination of women, I would remind you that what was at issue there had to do with tradition. In the present case, the issue is one of morals. So, I will modify my request: Can you offer a precedent where morals were the issue?

- The mission statement of Christ Church says that we respect the dignity of every person. But this causes me to wonder. How shall we treat willfully and persistently unrepentant sinners like this Robinson creature?
- If the doctrine of marriage is sacred, which we have always believed is between a man and a woman, how can it ever be trumped by unity?
- Can homosexuals ever be desirable role models as clergy? If not, why would we elect them as bishops?
- Those who oppose homosexuality in the church are often said to be homophobic. If we are to stay together, we need to take each other at face value.
- We need a clear statement of the extent to which we still rely on scripture. How does one pick and choose what to believe about the Bible?
- The Church is the only institution left that gives individual specific guidance about life's choices. Is it abandoning that role? How can it speak with authority if it is making up morals as it goes along?
- I am a life-long member of Christ Church and I am gay. What about me? What do you find so wrong?
- My son in high school has just told his mother and me that he is gay. We are searching for help. We accept him and hope the church will also. This is a very personal and important issue with me.

THE RESPONSE OF THE ANGLICAN COMMUNION

The election and consecration of Bishop Robinson by the Episcopal Church USA created immediate consternation among many of the 38 Primates in the Worldwide Anglican Communion. The Archbishop of Canterbury established The Lambeth Commission in October 2003 at the request of dissenting Anglican Primates. It requested venues for greater communication and understanding on issues that threaten to divide the world fellowship. The Commission, led by the Most Reverend Dr. Robin Eames, Archbishop of Armagh, Ireland, issued *The Windsor Report* in 2004.

Many in the Anglican Communion expressed dismay and disappointment on two levels at the action of General Convention. First, most of the church bodies rejected the consecration of Bishop Robinson and pointed out that this made him a bishop everywhere in the Anglican world. They acknowledged that the consecration cannot be undone, even though some Primates believe it is inappropriate to accept him. They were also disturbed that the American Church took this action without sufficient consultation with other parts of the Communion.

The Anglican Church, particularly in some parts of Africa, demanded that the American Church apologize for breaking faith. We were asked to refrain from ordaining other homosexual persons or permitting same-gender marriage blessings until the matter is resolved. In response, the American Episcopal Bishops decided to broaden the requested mandate and forgo consecration of all bishops until the next General Convention, thereby standing in solidarity with Bishop Gene Robinson. The Presiding Bishop on behalf of the Church expressed regret for the pain that had been caused to others, but noticeably did not express regret for the action taken in consecrating Bishop Robinson.

In the summer of 2005 the Presiding Bishop of the Episcopal Church made a formal response to the Windsor Report in the document titled, *To Set Our Hope on Christ*. He acknowledged the desirability of acting in concert and with full consultation with others in the worldwide Anglican Communion. Yet he defended the decision of his Church when it recognized the Rev. V. Eugene Robinson as a qualified priest who displayed in his life and ministry the fruits of the spirit, which were perceived as evidences of holiness. Finally, he pointed to a long appendix that chronicled the 40-year history of the struggle in reaching an understanding on homosexuality and the church.

Today's gay/lesbian movement has focused our attention and caused us to reassess our understanding of God's will as seldom before. The chapters that follow are offered as a defense of the position taken by General Convention in 2003. But first we review how the same struggle is unfolding in other mainline denominations.

UNITED CHURCH OF CHRIST (UCC)

The United Church of Christ is a union between the Congregational Church and the Evangelical Reform Church with 1,400,000 members. The UCC can best be described as a grass-roots denomination with power flowing up from the local congregation to denominational cooperative programs.

The 25th General Synod of the United Church of Christ met in Atlanta, Georgia from July 1-5, 2005. This Synod made an epic decision in support of gays, lesbians, bisexuals and transgender persons. First the church affirmed that it has been in the forefront of the struggle for justice and equality and for 30 years each General Synod adopted resolutions of support for homosexual persons. They had affirmed that Jesus' call to love your neighbor as yourself provides the mandate for equality in heterosexual marriages and the rationale for inclusion of gays and lesbians. They recognized that lesbians and gays have been marginalized in church and society and this reality does not comport with what justice requires.

The UCC builds its theology around the covenant made with God and one another. A resolution at this decisive Synod declared that covenant is central in the message of scripture concerning relationships and community. The overriding message of the gospel covenant is that God calls people to live fully the gift of love in just, mutually fulfilling relationships.

The text notes that covenant values do not depend on a single form of relationship. Some biblical texts encourage celibacy, forbid divorce, or require women to be subservient to men. Others forbid homosexual practice as it was then known. These are not authoritative because they are primarily expressions of cultural norms of the ancient Middle East. Rather, the authentic biblical model is found in Jesus' call for love and justice in all relationships. The church in official session affirmed that all human beings are created in the image of God, including persons of all sexual orientations. It follows that persons with same-gender orientation, whose sexuality is a gift from God, "have the right to lead lives that express their love, mutuality, commitment, consent and pleasure."

The resolution continued, "BE IT RESOLVED: that the twenty-fifth General Synod calls upon congregations to prayerfully consider adopting Wedding Policies at their churches that do not discriminate against gay or lesbian couples."

The resolution moved then to the political order with this statement: "LET IT BE FURTHER RESOLVED: the Twenty-fifth General Synod urges congregations and individuals to prayerfully consider and support state and national legislation to grant equal marriage rights to couples regardless of gender and to work against legislation, including constitutional amendments, to deny civil marriage rights to gay and lesbian couples."

The strong support for homosexual persons, relative to other denominations, can hide the opposition among the minority. The resolution of support recognized that the UCC is not of one mind and understands that in some churches it will be difficult to have a discussion of this issue. Yet the UCC voted down an alternate resolution that stated that marriage must be defined as between a man and a woman. The UCC honors local autonomy and recognizes that individual congregations can and will define their positions with varying levels of limited inclusion.

The UCC Coalition for Lesbian, Gay, Bisexual and Transgender Concern is officially recognized as a related, self-created organization. The Coalition supports affirmation of gays and lesbians in every facet of denominational life. It encourages formation of local chapters so that gays and lesbians can affirm and support each other as they integrate their lives into local congregations. The Coalition has participated actively in the study and discussion process over 30 years before the decisive vote in 2005.

PRESBYTERIAN CHURCH (USA)

This is the primary Presbyterian Church in the United States, a branch of the Protestant Reformation begun by John Calvin. The mainline denomination has a membership of 2.4 million in 11,000 congregations.

The Presbyterian Church (USA) is experiencing enormous conflict over whether to accept gays and lesbians in church and society. Many discerning insiders predict that the church will be split over the issue at the next General Assembly in 2006. A few propose "a gracious separation" into conservative and liberal denominations. Leaders are preoccupied with preventing such a separation and have formed a task force titled, "Peace, Unity and Purity" to once again study the issues surrounding homosexuality.

Church law as it now stands requires office holders to "live either in fidelity within the covenant of marriage between a man and a woman, or chastity in singleness." For the third consecutive General Assembly this law will be challenged. A proposal is being circulated to replace the marriage phrase "between a man and a woman" with "a covenant relationship between two persons."

We note that the Institute for Religion and Democracy has a chapter in the Presbyterian Church (USA) called "Presbyterian Action for Faith and

Freedom." Following the lead of the parent organization, a conservative "think-tank" outside of denominations, they claim to "defend and promote biblical values within the Presbyterian Church (USA)." IRD membership within the church claims that people feel excluded "by the dominant activist circles of the left." The Institute for Religion and Democracy advertises its avowed purpose of "reforming the church's social and political witness."

Two stories that appear on the national church website illustrate the quandary and the need for a new approach.

"Doug" remains anonymous out of fear of physical violence. He became a Presbyterian while a student at Ohio State University. He joined Knox Presbyterian in Hyde Park, Ohio. There he served as an usher, deacon and committee chair. In 1995 he was elected by the congregation as a representative to the Presbytery and was ordained as an elder. A person from his congregation later made an allegation before the Presbytery that Doug was gay. An investigation suggested that he admitted to being gay to friends and small groups in his church. His picture appeared in a Church Directory with another man who listed the same street address as Doug.

In June of 1996 Doug was brought before the Judicial Commission of the Cincinnati Presbytery. He stated that there had never been an issue about his gayness in his congregation. When asked why he had accepted the position of elder he replied, "when the church asks you to serve, you should try to say yes." He was convicted but the decision was reversed on a procedural issue and then referred back to the highest judicial court of the church where he was removed. His case created the circumstance around which the debate swirled.

In 1995 Martha Juillerat was serving as a Presbyterian minister. When she announced her sexual orientation and subsequent secret marriage to a woman, she was asked to resign her ordination at a meeting of fellow pastors in Kansas City, Missouri. Her testimony was that she felt called to pastoral ministry as a teen. She knew she was lesbian, but made a decision to follow church rules and live single and celibate. However, after several years she met a woman who became her partner. Later, they invited only four friends to a secret ceremony of holy union. Her partner had a serious bicycle accident in 1993 that nearly killed her. "After that," Martha said, "we decided that we could not stay hidden any more. We decided that was a sick way to live." She testified that leaving the ministry was the hardest decision she ever made.

Before resigning she requested gay and lesbian pastors or candidates for ministry to send her their liturgical stoles. She had hoped for as many as a dozen but she received 80 stoles, which she placed around the hall where her resignation service was conducted.

Her collection has grown to "a shower of stoles" totaling almost 800 from gay and lesbian priests and ministers in 13 denominations. She displays them at annual and regional meetings of churches. She commented, "Seeing the stoles is like seeing the Viet Nam memorial or the AIDS quilt. It helps take the issue out of people's heads and puts it into their hearts." The Shower of Stoles has now grown into a non-profit organization with a board of directors.

EVANGELICAL LUTHERAN CHURCH OF AMERICA (ELCA)

The Evangelical Lutheran Church of America, the largest sibling in a family of Lutheran churches in the United States has a membership of about 4.8 million. The ELCA is governed by a Constitution, By-Laws and Continuing Resolutions. These are amended regularly at Churchwide Assemblies. The latest edition is dated October 2005.

The denomination began on January 1, 1988, brought about by a union of three of the larger Lutheran bodies. Lutherans all recognize that their roots go deep into the life and teachings of Martin Luther and the Reformation soil.

The ECLA Churchwide Assembly is the national governing body that meets every four years. It has not escaped the intense debate over homosexuality. We note their 1995 Report on Human Sexuality that "gay and lesbian people, as individuals created by God, are welcome to participate fully in the life of the congregations of the ELCA." We pick up the story at the 2001 Assembly where the national body mandated that the Church engage in studies of human sexuality. The study had two parts. The first was to explore the blessing of same-gender unions and whether to consider lesbians and gays for ordained ministry. The second study was for the purpose of developing a general social statement on sexuality.

The mandate noted that some congregations are eager to engage in this exploration while others are hesitant. Those who developed the mandate "prayed that every member will share in this journey and that the end conclusion will be a faithful expression of our unity in Jesus Christ." The issues were carefully considered over the next four years in the working group that was appointed to write a draft report with recommendations for the Church Council. The working group had a paid fulltime Director who not only led the study but also spoke in churches and Synods across the country. The national Church Council, in turn, prepared legislative language to implement decisions, if they were made. These were distributed throughout the church prior to the Churchwide Assembly. Further, the Conference of Bishops weighed in with their advice on various options. The two mandates were folded into a single document.

The 2005 Churchwide Assembly considered three recommendations based on the study. The first passed as a simple majority vote. This general recommendation asked the church to give thanks for "the precious gift of unity and the richness of diversity" among ELCA churches. It asked that everyone respect the integrity of conviction and the weight of conscience among members who championed opposing views. The resolution asked members to find ways to live together faithfully in the midst of disagreement.

The second resolution passed with a small revision. It reaffirmed the traditional position, stated officially by the Conference of Bishops in October 1993, that "marriage is a lifelong covenant of faithfulness between a man and a woman." They concluded that there is no basis in scripture or tradition for establishing an official ceremony for the blessing of a homosexual relationship. "We therefore do not approve such a ceremony as an official action of this church's ministry." At the same time, the ECLA accepted those pastors and congregations that desired to be inclusive and minister to gay and lesbian persons. "Nevertheless, we express trust in and will continue dialogue with those pastors and congregations who are in ministry with gay and lesbian persons, and affirm their desire to explore the best ways to provide pastoral care for all gays and lesbians to whom they minister." The revision was for the removal of the words "gays and lesbians" leaving "pastoral care for all to whom they minister."

The third resolution explored whether the church wanted to go further and officially change its stance. Two positions were presented. The church had the options of accepting none, either or both. The first position in the resolution was to recognize the traditional biblical witness and standard for ministry but to make provision for exceptions. As divorced persons are now considered for ordination in the ECLA on a case-by-case basis, so gays and lesbians might be considered case-by-case. This resolution was supported by those who drew a parallel between divorce and homosexuality. Only clearly devout and well-prepared persons who evidence the fruits of the spirit would make it to ordination. The second provision of the resolution took the position that homosexuality is a condition and not a choice. Lifelong loving relationships should be encouraged and blessed in the union of gay and lesbian persons. The texts of scripture that condemn homosexuality were really condemning abusive relationships. The love ethic of Jesus is more central than particular passages in the Old Testament that form the legal structure of early Hebrew society.

Both parts of the third resolution were defeated. The

church is left with an official position that has no place for ordination or the blessing of same-gender unions, yet recognizes the deep difference in viewpoints and leaves open space for the minority to continue their ministry among gay and lesbian people. The issue promises not to go away. The ECLA prays that this ongoing disagreement will not overshadow the ambitious work of ministry and mission to which it is committed.

UNITED METHODIST CHURCH

The United Methodist Church is the second largest mainline Protestant denomination, after the Southern Baptists. The worldwide total membership is 11 million, with 8.6 million communicants in the United States. There are 34,892 local congregations in 504 Districts, served by 50 bishops.

The General Conference is the highest policy-making body at the international level and meets every four years. The last General Conference met in Pittsburgh, Pennsylvania in 2004. The next meeting is scheduled for Fort Worth, Texas in 2008.

The United Methodist Church has traditionally been committed to the Social Gospel. Its members have been active in abolition, women's suffrage, the rise of the labor movement, civil rights, and legislation that provides greater equality and emphasis on the needs of the poor. John Wesley, the founder, taught the doctrine of sanctification, or growth in holiness, including social holiness through acts of charity and social justice. Wesley placed the emphasis where Jesus did when he asked, "Though we may not all think alike, may we not all love alike?"

Every United Methodist General Conference since 1972 has sought to liberalize church policy toward gays and lesbians. To date the requisite number of votes has never been attained. The Book of Discipline declares homosexuality to be "incompatible with Christian teaching" and prohibits the ordination of "practicing, self-avowed homosexuals." It further "forbids clergy from blessing or presiding over same-sex unions," and forbids the use of UMC facilities for same-sex union ceremonies. Delegates from annual conferences on the east and west coasts support acceptance and inclusion; those in the south, the midwest and overseas outnumber them. The United Methodist Church, unlike other mainline denominations, counts all persons worldwide as members of the same Church. Hence, there is not a United Methodist denomination of Nigeria. Rather, United Methodists in Nigeria are members of the same United Methodist Church as those in Columbus, Ohio.

Many insiders believe that the national vote will evolve over time in favor of acceptance. However, the international membership is growing faster than membership in the United States and most of that overseas church, especially in Africa, is against making changes. Indeed some countries, including Nigeria and Iran, threaten homosexual transgressors with capital punishment, typically in accord with Islamic beliefs. A wide difference exists in these countries between official policy and concrete enforcement, yet the cultural sentiment strongly condemns homosexuality and United Methodist churches are a part of that milieu.

Church discipline in the UMC is enforced through decisions of the Judicial Council. Two recent decisions have stirred intense debate within the denomination. The Rev. Beth Stroud, a minister in Pennsylvania, is in an openly lesbian relationship. Meeting in Houston, Texas in October 2005, the Judicial Council upheld the removal of ministerial credentials from the associate pastor, although she is still providing leadership in the same congregation without benefit of ordination.

A second recent case stirred even more amazement. The Judicial Council found in favor of the Rev. Ed Johnson who had denied membership in his parish in South Hill, Virginia to a man who was in an openly homosexual relationship. The pastor had been placed on temporary leave by the Virginia Annual Conference but he was reinstated by the Judicial Council, ruling that as pastor he is within his right to exclude any person at his sole discretion.

Alarm bells are sounding throughout the church as a result of this ruling. Bishops and other church leaders point out that United Methodists have always stood for inclusiveness. The church includes and welcomes persons of all races, cultures and ages. Most assumed that homosexual persons are also welcome.

One expression of dismay was a "Worship Service of Thanksgiving and Protest" in Minneapolis at Hennepin Avenue United Methodist Church, held on November 20, 2005. An overflow attendance of 1,200 persons participated in an affirmation of lesbian, gay, bisexual and transgender persons and extended an apology "for this latest example of bigotry in the United Methodist Church." The Rev. Bruce Robbins, Senior Minister, said in the sermon, "I found this decision contrary to our denomination's constitution which affirms that all persons are of sacred worth and are eligible to attend worship services, participate in programs, receive the sacraments, and upon taking vows, become members."

The United Methodist bishops have weighed in on the debate. The Council of Bishops wrote in a November 2, 2005 statement that while parishes are responsible for discerning readiness for membership, "homosexuality is not a barrier." They cited the denomination's "Social Principles, which state that God's grace is available to all and that the church is committed to being in ministry with all persons."

The *Christian Century* magazine carried an almost unprecedented two-page advertisement paid for by the Iliff School of Theology. The ad was a letter to "The People of the United Methodist Church," endorsed by some 150 professors in United Methodist Schools of Theology. The message was clear and unequivocal: "We stand with the denomination's bishops, who declared 'homosexuality is not a barrier' to church membership. As theological educators responsible for assisting the church in the preparation of pastors and other Christian leaders, particularly in the United Methodist Church, we respectfully request an immediate reversal of their (Judicial Council's) action, lest the witness and service of the Body of Christ be further harmed."

The letter went to the theological heart of the matter: "Theologically, the very being of the church requires the inclusion of God's people at every level of the church. Inclusiveness is not a theological option or simply beneficial. The 'koinonia' fellowship of the Holy Spirit is violated when some Christian believers are excluded, stigmatized, and suffer discrimination because of the church's teachings and actions." The letter continued, "The sins of stigmatization and discrimination are immoral actions and attitudes contrary to the Word of God in Jesus Christ."[1]

But those who support the Virginia pastor point out that the same Book of Discipline holds the practice of homosexuality to be incompatible with Christian teaching and it bars the performance of same-sex unions by the church's clergy or in the church's sanctuaries. Two retiring members of the Judicial Council, Sally Askew and Sally Geiss, whose terms ended in 2004, sent a memo to United Methodist Communications asking that the denomination's slogan of "Open Hearts, Open Minds, Open Doors" be discontinued. They made the request on the grounds that "such language is false advertising." They made their point, even though the Communications department decided to continue the advertising campaign.

The Institute on Religion and Democracy is active in the United Methodist Church through a United Methodist Action Committee directed by Mark Tooley. The Institute works across denominational lines. It has generous amounts of conservative funding to destroy the progressive social gospel message wherever it is sounded. In more recent times, their primary effort has been to counter the movement toward inclusion. This organization has a specific agenda "to keep gay and lesbian people out of our church," said a leading UMC executive. Some question whether their fingerprints might be on the rulings by the Judicial Council. This is the same organization that shares office facilities and common sources of funding with the Anglican American Council, the group that is trying to organize Episcopal churches to reverse the rulings on homosexuality. If that movement is unsuccessful they propose that parishes leave the denomination.

Finally, the Rev. Troy Plummer, Executive Director, Reconciling Ministries Network, the unofficial United Methodist group advocating for full inclusion of lesbians, gays, bisexuals and transgender persons, said his organization is waiting for a prophetic statement calling for full participation. The letter from seminary faculty members is a giant step in that direction.

AMERICAN BAPTIST CHURCHES

American Baptists have 1,417,543 members in 5,555 churches. They are serious about their historic polity that claims that ultimate power resides in the local congregation. The General Board of the American Baptist Churches adopts policy by a three-fourth' majority, while resolutions are adopted by a two-thirds majority. A resolution representing the position of the ABC must call for some type of implementation and must be based on a policy statement. At a biennial "Meeting of American Baptist Churches," resolutions gauge the opinion of delegates and are called "Statements of Concern." However, no resolution at a national meeting is binding on a local congregation. A General Board policy document is only binding on the national staff.

The debate over homosexuality has proceeded in several forums. In August 2005, the Senate of the denomination's Ministers Council voted 32 to 30 to reject a requirement that would have barred practicing homosexuals from Senate membership. This is the only venue where their vote had authority. In November 2004 the Regional Executive Ministers Council voted 20 to 3 to refrain from recommending practicing homosexuals for leadership positions at the regional or national levels and for these denominational leaders not to participate in performing same-gender marriage ceremonies.

In June 2005, a national "Consultation Statement on Mission and Ministry" reviewed the history of the debate: "Today we have deep divisions around our understanding of Biblical interpretation, human sinfulness, and the potential of ministering together."

Most recently, in November 2005, the American Baptist General Board met at their Conference Center at Green Lake, Wisconsin. After committing to follow Jesus as a people of prayer, purpose and passion, and renewing their commitment to radical discipleship, the Region of Indiana and Kentucky brought a petition to amend a document titled, "We are American Baptists." They added words that described themselves as Biblical People "who submit to the teachings of Scripture that God's design for sexual intimacy places it within the context of marriage between one man and one woman, and acknowledge that the practice of homosexuality is incompatible with Biblical teaching." The amendment passed by a vote of 59 to 45, but it is only binding on those who voted.

This region is openly threatening to withdraw from American Baptist Churches. Another of the church's 35 regions, the Pacific Southwest, has already begun the process of separating from ABC, USA.

American Baptists Concerned is an Association of Welcoming and Affirming Baptists. They formed in 1972 as a voice for justice with the goal of bringing good news of inclusiveness and affirming love to American Baptist churches. Another cooperative organization of 40 churches has declared that each of them is openly supportive of gay and lesbian inclusion.

The polity structure for American Baptists makes it impossible for a national decision on homosexuality that is binding on churches. Those that are uncomfortable with the unsettled environment have the option to lead individual congregations or—if they can form consensus—entire regions out of the denomination. It appears that a movement is forming to do just that.

REFORMED CHURCH IN AMERICA

The Reformed Church in America is a relatively small denomination of 300,000 members. However, no denomination has wrestled more bravely with the angel of God than this oldest Protestant Church in North America. The early Dutch settlers organized a congregation in 1628 in what would become New York City.

Wesley Granberg-Michaelson leads this denomination. He regularly seeks to focus its concern on poverty and justice for the poor and away from division over homosexuality. He notes that a true reading of scripture would dictate such an emphasis, as more than 2,000 verses address this subject of justice for the poor to a mere handful of inconclusive verses on homosexuality. The denomination is engaged in a study of human sexuality with the goal of reaching some kind of consensus.

They concluded in an earlier study that "the climate of the church is to be receptive, gentle, and humble." A

1997 study guide called "Homosexuality: Seeking the Guidance of the Church" noted that the way churches have dealt with homosexuality "is mostly a story of ignorance, ineptitude and ill will...The church should acknowledge its sins against homosexual persons" and make a concerted effort to understand them. The Guide has been updated and is still in use.

Nonetheless, in 2004 the General Synod voted "to affirm that marriage is properly defined as the union of one man and one woman to the exclusion of all others." Many are unhappy with that position. Some say they cannot imagine working for the growth of churches or being part of them if they exclude some of God's children from the RCA family. Others with equal conviction cannot imagine why the church continues to debate the issue that has such clear biblical direction against homosexuality.

ROMAN CATHOLIC CHURCH

The apparent struggle within the Roman Catholic Church is over how to rout out gays from schools of theology that prepare men for ministry. The Congregation for Catholic Education, the Vatican department in charge of seminaries, released a six-page "Instruction" at the end of November 2005.

The document says that "the Church, while profoundly respecting the persons in question, cannot admit to the seminary or to holy orders those who practice homosexuality, present deep-seated homosexual tendencies, or support the so-called 'gay culture'." The Instruction adds that men can become priests if their "homosexual tendencies...were only the expression of a transitory problem—for example, that of an adolescence not yet superseded." But those for whom homosexuality is deep-seated "find themselves in a situation that gravely hinders them from relating correctly to men and women."

For centuries many men went into the priesthood because they found themselves to be gay. The Church taught that the only faithful response to God by gay men was to be celibate. So they entered the priesthood to fulfill life as a gay celibate. Now that rationale is called into question. The "Instruction" bars persons who have "deep-seated homosexual tendencies." The issue has moved from action to being. It is no longer just a matter of what a person does; the underlying issue has become who the person is.

The ruling explains that persons may be accepted for the priesthood if they overcome the tendencies toward gayness and can document their cure for at least three years. The accompanying explanation notes that the Church considers homosexuality a "disorder." Persons with a gay orientation, they conclude, are not capable of living emotionally mature lives. Homosexuality is not a gift from God but rather a psychological disorder that they must overcome. Homosexual acts are intrinsically evil.

The ruling is under-girded by theology. Christ is the groom; the Church is the bride. The clergy of the Roman Catholic Church today represent Christ as groom. A gay priest does not have that ability to represent the groom and therefore he should not be a priest. Should the Church go a step further and rule that all gay priests must leave holy orders, the impact on the supply of clergy would be even more devastating than it is now.

The ruling does go a step further. The Vatican has told bishops that gay priests should not teach in Roman Catholic seminaries. The accompanying letter sent to bishops does not question the validity of the ordination of gay priests who are celibate. But it adds, "Because of the particular responsibility of those charged with the formation of future priests, they are not to be appointed as rectors or educators in seminaries." Roman Catholic legal scholars note that the letter does not have the official weight of the Instructions.

The Rev. Donald B. Cozzens, a Catholic author and former seminary rector who now does survey research, indicates that a fourth to half of all U.S. Catholic priests are gay. He wondered in an interview with a Washington Post writer, Alan Cooperman, about bishops who happen to be gay. Cozzens noted that the Instruction "doesn't say that rectors or professors in our seminaries who have already been appointed should be removed, but one wonders if that's not what might begin to happen— kind of culling of gay rectors and professors." Cozzens proclaimed the Instruction to be a "bombshell" because it affects current priests and not just future ones. The Rev. Ladislas Orsy, a canon lawyer at Georgetown University, said the letter is only advice and not legislation. He noted that "we have a sweeping principle in canon law that no rule is retroactive unless it specifically says so."[2]

Although each bishop has latitude in how he applies the directive, the fallout will reach thousands of Catholic schools and parishes as gay men who are considering the priesthood, and some who have already been ordained, reevaluate their place in the Church. Every gay seminarian faces a question of conscience and at best an uncertain future as a Roman Catholic priest.

SUMMARY AND CONCLUSION

The United Church of Christ has wrestled with God and prevailed, moving their denomination toward a shared vision of justice for all persons and extending a warm welcome to gay and lesbian persons. The UCC followed two years after the Episcopal Church took its courageous stand and then went further in giving full support to same gender marriage, which the Episcopal Church withheld "for the sake of harmony." That issue will be on the agenda at General Convention of the Episcopal Church in 2006.

Other denominations still wrestle with God and most are becoming acutely crippled from the intense struggle. The official position of the Roman Catholic Church appears to have regressed to the point where struggle gives way to blind dogma.

Chapter 2
AFFIRMING INCLUSION

> Christ is the good shepherd
> Who knows and cares for every one of the
> sheep in his fold.
> In Christ there is neither Jew nor Gentile;
> In Christ there is no discrimination of gender,
> class or race.
> In Christ the poor are blessed, the simple
> receive that hidden from the wise.
> —Eucharistic Liturgy, *New Zealand Prayer*
> *Book*

The Rt. Rev. V. Gene Robinson was invited to preach the 200th anniversary sermon of the ordination of Absalom Jones, the first African-American priest ordained in the Episcopal Church. The date was February 9, 2004 and the place was St. Edmund's Episcopal Church in Chicago. In the sermon Bishop Robinson told a story which illustrates the case for inclusion.

Four American soldiers fought together in World War I. During their time in the trenches they became close friends. One was killed. The other three found a way to take his body back a few miles to a village where there was a Catholic Church, which had a beautiful cemetery with a fence around it. The soldiers went to the priest and asked that their buddy be buried in the cemetery. The priest asked, "Was he baptized?" The three comrades didn't know. They had talked about many things, but they never discussed baptism. The priest responded, "I'm sorry, you won't be able to bury your companion in the cemetery, but I will let you bury him just outside the fence at the corner."

After the war was over, just before shipping back to America, the three soldiers went back to the village to visit the grave of their fallen friend. They searched for the grave in vain. So they contacted the priest and asked what had happened. The priest said, "Very soon after you left, I got to thinking about what I had done and how horribly I had treated you three soldiers. And so I had the fence moved to include your friend."

Bishop Robinson concluded they moved the fence when Absalom Jones was ordained, and it was moved again when he was consecrated as a bishop.

CHOICE OR GIVEN

There are a few critical questions which form the crux of disagreement between persons who honestly find it necessary to exclude gays and lesbians from full participation in church and society and those who believe they should be accepted and supported. We build our cases based on these critical differences. The first is whether homosexuality for most persons is chosen or is given.

We who believe homosexuality is a given contend that children discover, usually at an early age, at least by puberty, that they are different. They then go through a long process of turmoil as they come to grips one way or another with their sexuality. The condemnation of parents, the conventions of society, the scorn and physical dangers, and the teachings of the churches all conspire to drive most homosexual youth into silence, secrecy and outward conformity. Nobody wants to be labeled "queer" or be reminded that the name most often used for them is "faggot," a name for the wood used when homosexual persons were once burned at the stake.

Research continues in an effort to isolate a genetic component or pinpoint a brain hormone to explain homosexuality. These links have not yet been verified but the evidence is growing. The strongest support for our view, however, is the testimony of homosexual persons in overwhelming numbers who say they inherited or at least discovered their same-gender orientation.

At the same time it should be made clear that nobody believes that all persons who practice homosexual acts are "hard-wired." There is a range within human sexuality that includes bi-sexual persons and some with stronger tendencies toward homosexuality who can still function as heterosexuals. There are those, such as prisoners, who engage in homosexual acts because of convenience or circumstance. Our claim is that for an overwhelming majority, probably 90%, homosexuality is a biological given.

Researcher Charles Rosetti at Oregon State University has been studying homosexuality in sheep for a decade. His studies lead him to conclude that sexual orientation is largely hard-wired into sheeps' brains before birth. He says that ranchers have long known that about eight percent of rams never father offspring because they have no sexual interest in female sheep. Australian sheepherders call them "shy breeders." Rosetti's male-oriented rams constantly ignore females and bestow amorous attention on males. He is now doing laboratory research by injecting heterosexual rams with a different hormone balance in an effort to produce more homosexual males in the herd. Last year he found that a brain region linked with sexual behavior was twice as big in heterosexual as homosexual rams. The gay rams also had lower levels of an enzyme that activates testosterone and promotes typical male sexual behavior.[3] This account is one of many studies in progress and is not meant to offer scientific proof of hard-wire pre-natal sexual determination in humans.

To cite another study, back in 1995 two scientists at the National Institutes of Health in Bethesda, Maryland experimented with fruit flies by transmitting a single gene into the male flies that caused them to exhibit intense homosexual behavior. The scientists claim to know a related gene in human beings, although there is no evidence yet that the human gene has an effect on sexual preference. We confess with frustration that solid proof has not yet been established in humans.

Opponents of this position believe that homosexuals are usually enticed into the lifestyle. By being naturally curious some individuals experiment with same-gender encounters and then become addicted to homosexuality. These opponents insist that all contact with homosexuals should be avoided by those who recognize their own same-gender desires. To the extent that the condition is unconscious, opponents contend that it is formed in the home where a boy's mother has been overprotective and his father has been distant or overbearing. They believe that homosexuals can be "cured," much like drug addicts or alcoholics can be cured, by prayer, determination, and counseling. They also maintain that a society that lets down its guard toward homosexuality will become promiscuous in permitting the spread of this evil. For opponents, homosexuality defies the natural male-female order of creation and must be opposed. They make no room for the innate variety that others of us believe exists within the human species.

There is a type of counseling termed "reparative therapy" that claims to treat homosexuality and provide a cure. The claim will be discussed in another context later. Here it is useful to say that the concept goes back to the work of a British theologian and self-proclaimed psychologist, Elizabeth Moberly. She wrote two books that are widely read by those who have a religious imperative to show that homosexuality is a chosen life-style. The easiest to read is titled *Homosexuality: A New Christian Ethic*.[4] Significantly, her research involved no subjects. She simply reviewed the writings of three dated works of Irving Bieber, Lawrence Hotteras and Sigmund Freud and then came up with the theory of Reparative Therapy. Moberly believes that the young boy fails to bond properly with his father and becomes estranged. At puberty he mistakenly seeks fulfillment with men in search of his missing father. Ex-gay and anti-gay groups from across the country flocked to hear her message and learn how to overcome homosexuality.

The Family Research Institute located in Colorado Springs, Colorado is dedicated to disproving that gayness is a biological given rather than a choice. The Chairman, Paul Cameron, claims numerous documented cases to prove homosexuals can revert to heterosexuality. An example given in their literature is of a 25 year old man who had his first sexual experience at age 13. His lesbian mother arranged for him to have a sexual encounter with an older gay man. Subsequently, his lifestyle was homosexual until he was distressed by public disapproval and personal loneliness. After reparative therapy his sexual orientation has become heterosexual. In rebuttal, we respond that he is probably one of those minority persons who did have the capacity and desire to exercise his heterosexual personhood, or perhaps he was a heterosexual person encouraged to become a practicing homosexual.

Another organization that promotes reparative therapy is "Focus on the Family," headed by James Dobson. He, too, calls homosexuality a "chosen" lifestyle. Both of these groups hold one-day seminars across the country, directing their appeal primarily to evangelical Christians. Persons who are "cured" come and testify. Persons who appear as experts tear down the scientific studies that seek to find a genetic or hormonal cause. The programs are packaged with slick literature and those who attend are sent out to save family life in America.

All of the major professional associations, on the other side, oppose reparative therapy. The American Psychiatric Association concluded in 1999 after careful study, "There is no published scientific evidence supporting the efficacy of reparative therapy as a treatment to change one's sexual orientation. The potential risks of reparative therapy are great, including depression, anxiety and self-destructive behavior." The American Psychological Association had said in 1998, "The reality is that homosexuality is not an illness. It does not require treatment and is not changeable." Added to these testimonies are the official positions of virtually all other professional organizations. Among others who believe homosexuality is a healthy and natural condition is the American Medical Association, which stated officially that it "opposes the use of reparative or conversion therapy that is based on the assumption that homosexuality is per se a mental disorder or based on a prior assumption that the patient should change his/her homosexual orientation." Official statements by the American Academy of Pediatrics, the National Association of Social Workers, and the American Association of School Counselors agree with the others.

Most lesbian and gay persons are sure they were born as homosexuals. The major professional organizations that work with homosexual persons agree. Despite the weight of professional opinion, perhaps as many as seventy-million conservative Christians in the United States believe that homosexuality is chosen, unnatural, sinful, and can be changed by reparative therapy, prayer and self-determination. These opponents believe that lesbians and gays should be kept away from straight youth and should be denied employment as school teachers. All mention of homosexuality should be eliminated from the curriculum and support groups for gay and lesbian youth should be forbidden. These are necessary measures, they feel, to shield young people from the temptation to enter lesbian or gay lifestyles.

A central question for the reader is to determine which of these assumptions is correct. Those who have a strong biblical or theological predisposition against homosexuality dismiss evidence that points to it as a given. Those who seek the acceptance of society have a strong desire to prove that homosexuality begins in the genes or brain hormones. Opponents claim there is no gay gene or it would have been found. Proponents say the human genome is extremely complex and study may take years more to unravel these mysteries. The issue is important in molding public opinion. A Pew Research phone survey in 2003 reported that 50% of people who think sexual orientation is fixed at birth support gay marriage, compared to only 20% who think it is a preference.

At the civil level, we as a nation must decide how to treat gay and lesbian persons. Should they be excluded from civil benefits of marriage when they form permanent unions? Is it appropriate for society to protect their basic human rights? Or, should we ostracize them and exclude them in every way possible to protect society from the evil they represent? Is that constitutional, given that our Bill of Rights was designed in part to protect the unpopular minority and the liberties of us all? These are important questions that we will answer at the ballot box, in the courts, and in our churches. Those who oppose lesbian and gay rights are organized and have amassed huge amounts of money to further their cause.

UNDERSTANDING SCRIPTURE

A second assumption is within the sphere of Christian faith. The issue is whether the Bible is an "inerrant," literally infallible collection of books in which every word has equal weight as a pronouncement from God. Most clergy and a good proportion of laity in the Episcopal Church reject inerrancy. This conclusion is based on biblical scholarship, scientific enlightenment and the teachings of Jesus. Those of us with this perspective have great reverence for scripture and believe its teachings are foundational. All scripture provides inspiration, guidance and reveals the ways of God. But we stumble into a sinkhole with no handle to pull ourselves out if we say that all scripture is inerrant, given literally by God, to be believed without question. As we shall learn later, Jesus dealt precisely with this issue in the Hebrew Bible. He rejected inerrancy and taught a new way to understand these scriptures. It was to apply the love principle to each law and to see if it measured up. Much of Jesus' profound disagreement with the priests, Pharisees and other religious types in his society was over this issue.

To follow Jesus in rejecting a literal interpretation of the Bible does not mean that it is less important to us. We do not need to slip into subjectivity in which "anything goes" when we use the Jesus principle of interpretation. Rather, it calls us to a higher standard, as we measure Old Testament laws by the mind of Christ. It also calls us to greater responsibility because we then take on the task of being agents, "responsible selves" using the principle of love to weigh and balance ethical decisions, rather than follow a prescribed divinely ordained law or scripture verse. It is exhilarating to be part of God's unfolding revelation for our time. We follow a God who is at work among us, rather than a God who binds us to ancient inhumane prescriptions.

EMBRACING THE AGE OF SCIENCE

A third assumption is that "the enlightenment" is also a part of God's revealed truth. We know a great deal about the age of the earth, the way the stars and galaxies are formed, the laws of physics, chemistry and other aspects of the physical universe. We find evidence for biological evolution, and we now have greater understanding of disease and the human body. The age of science has supported life to make it better. Our knowledge is far from complete but it is light years ahead of where it was when the Bible was written. Those who believe in the inerrancy of scripture face the problem of reconciling pre-scientific knowledge of biblical times with known science of today. God is the author of science. The knowledge we have reveals the way God created and enhanced human life. Accepting the truths of science in no way invalidates our trust in God, the creator and redeemer of the world.

The book of Genesis was a profound theological account of God's creation. It reveals humanity's endowment with God-like qualities expressed in human intelligence, creativity and love. Also the story explains how humanity is marred by unspeakable wrong-doing toward God, the creative order and other people. We accept that account, not as history, but as myth, as the Hebrew story of creation. We believe that such a story provides the most profound way to express reality. We also believe that it is mistaken piety to insist that the world and all living things were literally created in seven days and that the earth is somewhere between six and ten thousand years old, based on genealogies as recorded in the Bible.

Our method of interpretation is important as we approach the issue of homosexuality. We are not bound by an ancient understanding of sexuality. Nor are we subject to tribal customs of ancient Hebrew society. We do not dishonor our biblical ancestors when we disagree with their assessment of homosexuality. We do not betray God, whose very name is "The Truth," when we affirm a new truth revealed to us, when we find a new appreciation for the validity of lesbian and gay persons based on the profound love of Jesus for all people.

These basic assumptions within the Church form the background context for a biblical perspective on homosexuality. As noted in the previous chapter, the Episcopal Church has grappled with the issue of homosexuality for the last forty years. At the last General Convention in Minneapolis in 2003, by a larger than the required vote of clergy, laity and Diocesan Bishops, they agreed to the election and consecration of one of its gay priests to the position of bishop. The Church said in effect that it accepts homosexuality as the way God made some people, not as a sinful perversion. This human condition is not inherently sinful. Nobody should be excluded from the church, even its highest office, based on sexual orientation.

FACTORS LEADING THE EPISCOPAL CHURCH TOWARD INCLUSION

Why was the Episcopal Church the first major denomination to accept homosexuality as its official policy? In the last chapter we saw how other mainline denominations are also struggling with the issue of homosexuality. It is instructive to examine some of the special qualities and structures of the Episcopal Church that help answer this important question.

Within the Episcopal Church the honest grappling with homosexuality has this forty year history, as evidenced by study commissions, reports and resolutions. When debates were contentious and issues unresolved, the Church in Convention would send the issue back to local parishes for discussion with the hope of building consensus. In addition to the hard work of coming to understand homosexuality over a period of many years, the weariness that set in after facing the same issues one convention after another may have contributed, perhaps unconsciously, to the decision to elect Bishop Robinson.

Another important factor is the way the Episcopal Church functions at the national level. Power is shared broadly among bishops in the House of Bishops and among clergy and laity in the House of Deputies. Because a consensus must be formed, each listens and learns from the others. Further, lobbying is permitted and even encouraged. Each group with an interest in decisions of the Convention can bring its literature and distribute it. Each is free to lobby and make its case. This is understood as the way democracy is supposed to function. Those who represent an unpopular or minority position are not ostracized or shunted aside. Rather, they are heard with a degree of patience and if their arguments make sense, their cause will grow in acceptance over time.

An important organization that has lobbied and educated within the national church is Integrity, the national organization of gay, lesbian, bisexual and transgender persons.[5] Founded in 1974 by Dr. Louie Crew, and presently led by the Rev. Susan Russell, Integrity is present at each Convention, ready with its own resolutions, and quick to lobby deputies who might be open to persuasion. Integrity is known for its appeal to the conscience of deputies. Of course, many deputies, both clergy and lay, are homosexuals. Integrity also forms networks in dioceses and encourages local chapters or circles in congregations. The Church has been blessed to have such a vocal, persistent and astute presence to witness for the gay and lesbian community. Integrity is an arm of evangelism that has brought thousands of estranged homosexual persons back to parish life. These individuals, local groups and Internet communities serve as leaven in the Episcopal loaf.

An important strategic structure is the way the Episcopal Church in the United States of America owns property. In the Diocese of Virginia, for example, the vestry of each parish appoints Trustees who hold the property in Trust on behalf of the Diocese, for the Episcopal Church. This becomes important when the national church makes controversial decisions. Even though a majority of members favor the position on homosexuality taken at General Convention, there is a vocal and deeply distressed minority. The rectors and vestries of individual parishes, and in some instances of dioceses, threaten to leave the Church, or switch their allegiance to some bishop in the Anglican Communion in another country with whose position they agree. When this occurs the dissidents could be left with the looming challenge of buying or building new facilities for their new churches, although the Church has gone to great lengths to avoid such a final rift.

In the Episcopal Diocese of Lexington, Kentucky, the Rt. Rev. Stacy F. Sauls, Bishop, provides an example of a diocese that had a parish that refused to permit their bishop to come for his annual visit to confirm new Christians, to conduct baptisms, or to consult with parish officials. Parish leaders indicated their decision to withhold their assessments to the diocese and the national church. After extended consultations, when all creative efforts to reach compromise agreements had failed, the bishop notified the rector and communicants that on a given date they were being evicted. Bishop Sauls made it clear that an Episcopal priest cannot claim the authority of his or her ordination and at the same time denounce the Episcopal Church and seek to function in that church under the cover of a fictitious transfer to another part of the world. All who supported their bishop and the action of the Church were invited and urged to stay and help build a new congregation. On the first Sunday after the eviction the bishop gathered volunteers from several parishes to attend a liturgy in the building and celebrate the Eucharist. Beginning the next Sunday an entirely new congregation began to gather, mostly young adults. The first Sunday there were 14 present, the next Sunday 25, then 30. This new congregation has formulated a mission statement in which they pledge to strive for justice and peace and respect the dignity of every person, including gay and lesbian persons.

Finally, the event that made a decision necessary at General Convention in 2003 found focus in the person of the Rev. Canon V. Gene Robinson. He was the center of the controversy. His deep spirit-filled life and his outstanding ministry made him an ideal test case.

THE PIONEER PRIEST WHO BECAME BISHOP

The Rev. Robinson served for 15 years as Canon for the Diocese of New Hampshire, a position in which he was the administrator in assisting the bishop. He had moved to New Hampshire from the Diocese of Newark in 1975 and served as a parish priest until 1988. Some further background may be helpful in understanding the man who was first to break the barrier and become an openly gay elected bishop.

He was born in 1947 in a small town near Lexington, Kentucky. His mother had expected a girl baby and had picked a girl's name. At birth his parents were surprised that he was a boy, but it seemed not to matter because the doctor told the grieving parents that he was born paralyzed and would not live. They gave him the girl's name, Vicky Imogene, for the birth and death certificates. He outgrew the paralysis and went home to a humble tobacco sharecropper's house. He grew up in a warm Christian environment and was active in the Disciples of Christ church, where his brother and parents still worship.

The boy was acutely aware that his life had been spared and felt he had a special mission of service. In high school he dreamed of becoming a medical doctor who would save the lives of infants. After an outstanding high school experience he was offered a half scholarship to attend Princeton University and a full scholarship at the University of the South in Tennessee. The Episcopal College saw great promise in the young man and was ready to make a substantial investment in him. During his years at Sewanee, Gene Robinson joined the Episcopal Church and grew to love the liturgy, history, and message of the Church. He came to realize that God's call was not to medicine but to ordained ministry. He graduated cum laude and moved on to General Theological Seminary in New York.

The young man carried with him a terrible secret. He knew that he was gay, but he also knew that he could not admit his condition. He felt that to accept his homosexuality would be to destroy his career and lead him to suicide. At one point he said, "Suicide was something we thought the good homosexual did." While at General Seminary he determined to undergo a two-year extensive counseling program to help overcome his homosexuality. He met Isabella Martin while on an internship at the University of Vermont. After a courtship they discussed marriage. The theological student was completely honest and shared with her the fact that he was gay but was trying to live as a heterosexual. He explained that he was not sure it would work, but he would like to try. She agreed and said if later they were not able to continue successfully they would deal with the situation at that time.

Gene Robinson was ordained June 9, 1973. They married and served in the Diocese of Newark until receiving an appointment to a parish in New Hampshire two years later. By all accounts the new priest had a successful ministry. His wife's family owned a large farm in New Hampshire. They were given a small parcel of this land on which to open a girls' summer camp and a spiritual retreat center. The couple had two daughters, Jarnee and Ella.

After ten years as a "straight" priest the Rev. Robinson announced to his congregation that he was gay and that he and his wife were ending their marriage. He had been in intensive counseling and had also worked closely with his bishop before making the decision. The couple had discussed the matter thoroughly and decided that both of them could better find fulfillment in life by this decision, although they wanted always to be friends and partners in rearing their children. The couple went back to the parish where they were married and had a second ceremony, this time to relieve each other of the original vows and return their rings, but with the pledge to continue their role as parents and friends.

Bishop Robinson has recounted on many occasions how he was fearful that his ministry would be ended and perhaps he would be defrocked. He reached his decision to "come out" after intense struggle, prayer and counseling. He felt that to be honest with himself and others he had to declare his sexual orientation. He also believed that he needed the friendship and intimacy of a male partner in order to function at his best in ministry. He and his former wife maintain a cordial and caring relationship and he remains close to his children. His bishop, the Rt. Rev. Douglas E. Theuner, in 1988 invited Rev. Robinson to become his chief of staff as a canon. In that capacity of canon, he worked closely with parishes across the state on all manner of projects to support the diocese and to build up local congregations. Indeed, his ministry extended to the national church. In the 1990's he developed the "Being Well in Christ" conference model for The Cornerstone Project and led clergy conferences in more than 20 dioceses in the U.S. and Canada. He also initiated Fresh Start, a two-year mentoring program for all clergy in new positions in New Hampshire, and co-wrote the Fresh Start curriculum, now in use in nearly half of the dioceses of the Episcopal Church.

The Robinsons' daughters were ages eight and four at the time of their separation. He found a book in Denmark that told the story of a gay man explaining a separation and divorce to his daughter. The father and older daughter read the book together and he explained his sexual orientation. She ended by affirming him and saying she hoped he would find a partner who would make him happy. The two of them then read the book to the four year old girl. Both daughters wrote essays for college entrance about that night as a highlight, a most meaningful time in their lives. Within two years after the divorce Isabella remarried. A year later Canon Robinson met and formed a long-term partnership with a New Hampshire Civil Service official.

When Bishop Theuner announced plans to retire, the Diocese had the task of selecting a new bishop. Canon Robinson was nominated along with four other candidates. In fact, he had previously been nominated by the Diocese of Newark and the Diocese of Rochester. There was strong support in New Hampshire for electing their canon. People in the diocese had come to love him and appreciate his ministry. They expressed their conviction that since he was the strongest candidate they should elect him as the first openly gay bishop of the Episcopal Church. His election came on the second ballot, something that very seldom happens because a candidate must receive a majority from among the total number of candidates.

But before he could be consecrated, because of the calendar timing, he had to be approved by the Diocesan Bishops and the Deputies of the National Church at General Convention. (If the election had not come at a time close to General Convention, the approval process would have involved approval by a majority of Diocesan Bishops and a majority of Standing Committees of the Dioceses.) Many church leaders at the national level testified that they discerned in Canon V. Gene Robinson the marks of holiness in his life and ministry that are signs of a qualified bishop. They joined the people of New Hampshire in testifying that he possessed the "fruits of the Spirit," qualities of caring, gentleness, kindness and firm conviction that are signs of God's presence in a Christian. In short, he was a rather ideal candidate to break the ice and become the first openly gay bishop.

Bishop Robinson was present at General Convention. He spoke to deputies. He answered questions at press conferences. He freely opened himself to the scrutiny of those who made the decision. This happened in a highly charged atmosphere in which he was receiving death threats from outsiders. He later testified that he wore a cumbersome bulletproof vest and was barraged with outpourings of hatred.

At the ceremony when he was elevated to bishop, the death threats were present again. Bullet-proof vests, hidden under flowing robes, were worn by the Presiding Bishop, the candidate, and others who participated. One man in the procession who appeared to be clergy was actually a member of the police department, ever on the alert for displays of violence. The clergy and lay leadership in the diocese of New Hampshire shared in the tension and the danger. Following his official election his office staff was briefed on how to deal with bomb threats. For them it was a burden worth bearing in support of their new bishop.

The consecration ceremony was held in the University Sports Arena with 4,000 in attendance. Those who opposed the consecration were invited to speak. Assistant Bishop David Bena of Albany, New York spoke for 38 opposing bishops in the United States and Canada and stated they would not recognize him as a fellow bishop. Then 45 bishops laid hands on him while Presiding Bishop Frank Griswold recited the ancient prayer of consecration. Afterward the congregation burst into a three minute standing ovation. Bishop Robinson later was overheard to say, "The love spilling out of this place was phenomenal."

Without such a positive role model to humanize the debate, the vote at General Convention could have gone the other way. The die was cast for the Episcopal Church. Critics claimed that the church would lose many members and a major amount of financial support needed to sustain its national ministry and mission projects. They stated that the more the church has reached out to become inclusive, the more membership has declined. The writer notes that in his own parish, Christ Church in Alexandria, Virginia, one pledge of a million dollars to the building fund was rescinded and over $200,000 was withdrawn from annual pledges. One stalwart priest of another parish who supported the action said it was the right decision, "even if we end up with only twelve faithful disciples."

RELIEF AND REJOICING

The Church has been fractured by this decision, but financial support after initially dropping is now surprisingly strong and growing. Disagreement, tension and unrest are present but there is also a clear resolve and a sense of relief among many that the issue has been decided. And, of course, when one asks homosexual church members, the decision was like "manna from heaven." It was gospel for them, good news. It was a turning from death to life. It was a time to hear the angels singing "hallelujah."

Chapter 3
A PASTORAL PERSPECTIVE

> O Divine Master, grant that I may seek not so
> much to be understood as to understand....
> —St. Francis, ***Prayer for Peace***

For those with eyes to see, the landscape is strewn with human wreckage caused by society's rejection of gay and lesbian persons.

As pastor of a congregation, the clergy person has an obligation to minister both to gay and lesbian members and to the families of those who discover such persons within their households. Whatever position the church takes ultimately on same-gender marriage and on ordination of clergy and bishops, it recognizes and states clearly that all members are equally deserving of respect and pastoral care. As early as 1976 at General Convention the Episcopal Church resolved: "Homosexual persons are children of God who have a full and equal claim with all other persons upon the love, acceptance, and pastoral concern and care of the Church."

Many rectors want to go a step further and assist parishioners in dealing with their fears and misunderstandings concerning homosexuality. They also want to be proactive in helping their congregations understand and accept the position of their national Church.

MINISTERING TO HOMOSEXUALS AND HOMOPHOBES

The Church has a ministry of caring. Those who lead must be patient with members of their congregations. But we must balance our patience with our impatience for justice. After all, we also have a ministry of justice. How do we deal with that minority of members who express strong hostility against accepting same-gender persons? At a time when this issue threatens to disrupt our parishes, split our national Church, and sever ties within the larger Anglican Communion, it is time to form a strategy for expressing support for the Church.

The pastor will never get a grip on homosexuality in his or her parish until homophobia is also addressed. Homosexuality is a fact. An ever-larger number of gay and lesbian persons are gaining the courage to declare their identity and stand for their rights. In the metropolitan area of Washington, D.C. on June 12, 2005, the annual parade and festival celebrating gay and lesbian life was larger than ever before, with an estimated 100,000 persons, largely homosexual, participating.

Anxiety about homosexuality is also a fact. The more open and strident gays and lesbians become, the higher the level of anxiety. Many of us who are heterosexuals and who intellectually support gays and lesbians still have secret anxiety and harbor feelings of fear or disgust. Indeed, we find the subject difficult to discuss and therefore, discussions are often strained. This is also true, of course, of any conversation regarding sexuality.

Why does this issue stir such feelings? A good deal of the research now being conducted focuses on the causes for same-gender orientation. Little or no research has been done to determine the reasons for our repression, prejudice and even violence against homosexual persons. We worry over why men fall in love with men or women love women. Many of us spend enormous energy and erect high barriers to make sure such people feel unwelcome among us. But we rarely stop to ask why we have such intense feelings.

We are told that gay people are destroying traditional families. One in four homosexual young men and women is disowned by his or her family when sexual identity is revealed to mom and dad. Could the non-accepting parents be destroying the family?

Some observers believe that the heart of the problem is homophobia, not homosexuality. Homophobia is fear and hatred of homosexuals. These critics say the one in need of healing is the oppressor, not the oppressed. They remind us that it is always easy to blame the victim. Bishop Desmond Tutu took this position and compared it with his struggle against apartheid. "We struggled against apartheid because we were being blamed for something (our color) that we could do nothing about. It is the same with homosexuality. The orientation is a given, not a matter of choice. It would be crazy for someone to choose to be gay."[6]

United States Senator Robert C. Byrd grew up poor but proud in rural West Virginia. He was a member of the Ku Klux Klan in his early adulthood. Later, as a United States Senator his views changed dramatically. He recently wrote a reflection on his life and in the book he tried to understand his experience.

Yes, he watched one Saturday as a child while white hooded men wearing masks marched in Matoaha, West

Virginia, and he later learned that his coal-miner adoptive father was in the group. Yes, he got caught up with the idea of being in an organization to which "leading persons" belonged. But he concluded with these telling words, "Blacks were generally distrusted by many whites, and I suspect they were subliminally feared."[7]

The words "subliminally feared" probably explain a great deal of the homophobia related to homosexuality. Parents fear that gay men will seduce their sons into homosexual activity and lead them into a permanent gay lifestyle. Men fear that they, themselves, are not safe from potential advances by gays. Some receive sexual advances from gays and are frightened by the experience. Or, more likely, they are approached in their imagination. This undefined, deep-seated fear of the unknown helps to explain a great deal of the irrational behavior.

Of course, the pastor will not find it helpful to accuse opponents who support a principled biblical position of being homophobic, a condition that may or may not be true. In any event, name calling of opponents is not a helpful way forward. A more productive stance is to recognize how deeply ingrained in our collective unconscious and in our culture is our fear of homosexual persons. The pastor or parish teacher can aim to help all of us at least to become "recovering homophobes."

It is no secret among psychologists that often those persons who most fear homosexuality are themselves strongly drawn toward same-gender sexual relationships. To sustain their own resolve of remaining untainted they characterize gays and lesbians as abnormal, almost sub-human.

The state legislature in Maryland provided a

glimpse into the murky world of homophobia. The State considered and enacted a "Medical Decisions Law" that grants gays and lesbians the right to help make medical decisions for their partners if they prove their relationship and register ahead of time. Eleven thousand gay and lesbian couples voiced their support. An opponent of the bill, Minority Whip Anthony J. O'Donnell shared with legislative colleagues his own misgivings. He worried about his "baby daughter," even though she is 18 years of age. What if she got swept up in a romance with another woman and a register existed? She might decide to designate the lover as a partner for life because "kids that age think new friends are going to be friends for life." He concluded, "Her mother and I would no longer have any say."

The most successful way forward is to provide opportunities for parishioners to have personal experiences of living and working alongside openly gay and lesbian persons who are also committed Christians. For members of a local parish to share their personal stories can also be life changing. When one is permitted the privilege of living into the life of another who has endured rejection, pain, suffering and all kinds of injustice, and can still bear a testimony of faith and love for the church, the listener often feels that she or he is standing on holy ground.

A number of Episcopal churches in Washington, D.C. advertise in the **Washington Blade**, a weekly newspaper for the gay and lesbian community. A young man in his early 20's accepts the invitation, attends a Sunday liturgy and then decides that he is welcome and can cast his lot in life with the parish. He is invited at an appropriate time to share his story: "My father and mother have disowned me and said I was unclean. My older brother and my sister-in-law have asked me not to come to their house any more because they are afraid I will give AIDS to my niece and nephew. I am especially lonesome and depressed now that Christmas is coming...." He concludes, "You have no idea how hard it has been to be rejected by my two basic support systems, my family and my church. And you have no idea how grateful I am that you have welcomed me."

One is entitled to again raise the question, "Who is sinning?" Is it the young man who discovered his sexual identity and was honest enough to share it with his family, or is it the parents who disowned their son?

Alan Keyes, a conservative Christian political leader from Maryland, was a candidate for the United States Senate from Illinois in the 2004 election. Much of his campaign was built around "social issues" with opposition to homosexuality at the heart of his speeches. At each campaign stop he referred to the practice as "selfish hedonism." Mr. Keyes' 19-year-old daughter, Maya, revealed during this time that she is a lesbian. She has spoken publicly about what happened at home. She was told to get out of her father's house and she was completely cut off financially because of her sexual orientation.[8] However there is a brighter side to this dark story. A gay/lesbian group, The Point Foundation, awarded Maya a scholarship of $20,000 for her first year to attend Brown University.

Almost every priest and minister will have the opportunity to counsel parents of children who are homosexual. And their support for gay and lesbian youth at critical moments can make a great difference for the remainder of their lives. Pastoral support for both parents and youth can be a stabilizing force at a turbulent time. To quietly secure funds for help in college for a long-time youth group member who is cut off from family seems to be a sure sign of the kingdom.

Parents need pastoral care when by supporting their child they are condemned by others. Dr. Norman Kansfield was President of New Brunswick Theological Seminary, an old and honored school for training ministers in the Reform Church in America. He was reprimanded and then had his contract cancelled when he presided at the wedding of his lesbian daughter in Massachusetts. "We decided that the president had put the seminary in an awkward position by performing that ceremony without giving us the benefit of offering sufficient counsel," said a spokesman for the school. In a letter sent to the Board shortly before the June 19, 2005 ceremony, Dr. Kansfield informed the Board of his decision to preside at his daughter's ceremony and stated that he was not asking for permission.[9] This bold and principled action by a renowned churchman needs the affirmation and emotional support of a pastor and an understanding congregation.

When the clergy or lay person wants to be proactive and lead a parish in dealing with homosexuality, she or he might consider a first step that is personal and autobiographical. How did I become involved? What risk do I take in being honest on this issue? What kind of struggle did I face? In this ministry of reconciliation the clergy person's position is strengthened when she or he recognizes vulnerabilities and then shares the struggle to understand. Another helpful approach is to articulate the hurts, fears and misunderstandings of the victims, perhaps also members of the parish.

Youth leaders in the parish might want to discuss with high school students whether they would like to join others on a given day in a vow of silence at school to draw attention to discrimination and harassment that many gay, lesbian, bisexual and transgender students face in school each day. This annual program began after a sample survey of 1,000 gay and lesbian high school students reported that four out of five of them were harassed regularly. The survey showed further that 83% of the time teachers did not intervene when the epitaphs "faggot" or "dyke" were used in their presence. Four hundred fifty thousand students nationwide took part in such a recent "Day of Silence." Parish leaders do the work of the kingdom when they support a process of teaching respect for other races, religions, physical impairments or sexual orientation.

Consider several scenarios that could, without too much imagination, present themselves to a typical congregation.

The rector is preparing his Sunday homily in the church office when he gets a telephone call. The person on the other end of the line is a friend and fellow rector in another city. He states that a young woman whom he has been counseling is in his office. She is an active member of his parish. She is a lesbian, has "come out" and is struggling to find her way. The young woman is moving to his city and will be looking for a church home. "Can I count on your church?" is the friend's question. The rector prays in silence, "Father, let this cup pass from me," but says with as much cheer as possible, "Sure. Let me speak to her now." After a brief conversation he invites her to his church and sets up a time for them to meet.

The young woman keeps the appointment with the rector at her new home and presents her case. She is wary, fearful, yet determined to be herself. The rector pledges his personal support but warns that members are mixed in their views and some may have hostile feelings. He gives her the names of three or four persons in the parish who are gay or lesbian and suggests she contact them. He also gives her the address and phone number of Integrity, suggesting she might like to know more about this ministry among homosexual persons in the Episcopal Church.

In another setting, a youth minister shares with the rector that he is gay. The rector is determined to show respect for the staff member but there is also the task of dealing with the youth of the parish. Rightly presented, and with the support of approving parents, this can be an important moment of learning and acceptance for a person with a homosexual orientation.

Rumors and suspicions about a same-gender couple in the parish come to the attention of the priest. Is constructive intervention possible that will support the couple and alleviate the anxiety of the fellowship? Can the senior warden go quietly to key members of the parish and enlist their help in supporting the couple and thus set an example for others?

A gay organization requests use of the church facility for its meetings. Can this request be accommodated in the same way that Alcoholics Anonymous, Boy Scouts, and other groups are permitted to use facilities for a modest fee? Will the appropriate committee that deals with church property assume the responsibility and take the lead in a decision?

Gays and lesbians come for personal counseling, as do their parents and families. Can we provide helpful literature? Are we willing to give pastoral support and the affirmation that gayness is a gift from God? In any event, we must provide an honest, accurate assessment of the historic position of the church and the present official position of the denomination as well as that of the Anglican Communion. Whatever our position as clergy or lay leader, we are entrusted with the task of ministering with sensitivity to the deep feelings and needs of our parishioners.

In short, there is no longer a way for any church to avoid this issue, even if we wanted to. We can try to "keep the lid on" and ignore anything related to homosexuality. But, be assured, it will be done at the expense of the person needing a healing ministry. John Milton expressed the lament, "The hungry sheep look up and are not fed...." We surely have a pastoral obligation to see that our flock is, indeed, fed. We, as Episcopalians, now have the support of the national church to back the local leadership.

CONSTRUCTIVE CONVERSATION AT CHURCH

For the past forty years each General Convention has sought to deal prayerfully and constructively with homosexuality. When no agreement seemed possible, a resolution would be passed to take the matter back to the parish level and conduct discussions guided by the Holy

Spirit. It was hoped that through openness and listening to others the Church would find the guidance it sought. Perhaps, it was hoped, the truth that sets us free would rise from voices in the pews.

Indeed there are thoughtful people in the pews. Many of these saints of God see us expressing a split personality. On one side is a traditional rejection of homosexuality. On the other side, they know family and friends who are homosexual and who need and deserve the full support of the church. They would like to see the church take the lead in creating a just society in which such persons have equal rights and are equally respected. Just where and how do we at church connect the dots to make sense of this situation? This is a subject we should be discussing. As one person said, "We really do need a deep and mature conversation."

But when the hour arrives for such conversation it can readily become a confrontation. Too often the end result is hostility rather than honesty. People go away angry rather than enlightened. As a result, in part with a practical view to church finance, we find it easier to forego discussion on this topic and content ourselves by talking about something less controversial. The challenge for the leader is to help parishioners focus their anger at injustice rather than at each other.

How does the parish engage in constructive conversation? As on so many topics related to parish life, the Alban Institute has published a book that offers helpful guidance, ***Homosexuality: Dialogue on a Different Subject***.[10] Chapter 4 is titled, "Rules for Talking about It":

- Begin by finding and articulating areas of agreement.
- Avoid name calling, i.e. "homophobe," "queer," or "pervert."
- Represent the opposition fairly and accurately. It is hard to really listen.
- Distinguish the actor from the act. A good person may have a faulty position.
- Identify the core or central issues.
- Admit weaknesses in one's own position.
- Distinguish moral substance from a particular formulation.
- When summarizing, include the perspectives of all who contributed.

PERSONAL STORIES

We learn and grow by hearing and telling our personal stories. Here are true accounts of enormous suffering, even death, because of our attitudes toward gays and lesbians. They reveal the evil we do in the name of religion, often without even knowing it. These stories illustrate the destructive side of our attitudes of exclusion, even when the harm is unintended.

A woman, employed in the federal government, came to work one day in great distress. She shared her story with her supervisor. She had been dating a man for whom she had great respect, even love, but she came to realize that he was homosexual. He was never able, she said, to have a satisfactory sexual relationship with her, although he professed to love her. After much soul-searching she decided to break off the relationship. A week later the man committed suicide. Homosexuality was unacceptable to his family and to her, and heterosexual sexual relationships were not possible. His utter misery and rejection led to his death. The suicide rate among homosexual persons is from two to three times greater than in the national population. His death also left the woman feeling responsible and guilty.

Again, a professor at a theological seminary related how a middle-aged woman who was preparing for ministry came to class in great anguish. The professor and students were shocked when she reported that her teenage son had committed suicide. He was no longer able to deal with his sexual orientation. Again, thirty to forty percent of all teenage suicide can be attributed to rejection and anguish over homosexuality.

A lovely young woman full of joy and promise unknowingly married a homosexual man. Her parents were proud of his work as an historic restoration architect. In time he confessed he knew he was gay, but he wanted so much to have a "normal" life that he thought if he tried hard enough it would work out. And, of course, the young woman was left devastated and eventually she divorced him.

The Straight Spouse Network was born in 1986 on the West Coast to provide emotional support for straight partners when they are married to gay or lesbian persons. There are no official figures as to how many marriages include a gay, lesbian or transgender spouse, but this organization estimated from their phone calls and e-mails that recently they had been in contact with more than 9,000 straight spouses who are married to gay persons. This situation speaks to something very intrinsic and profound. Is not our rejection of homosexuality in society leading to mismatched and unfulfilled marriages? Is the breakdown of marriage due to homosexuality? Or is it the result of our refusal to accept it and support constructive paths for its expression?

The author's first experience of working with a group of gay and lesbian persons was between 1976 and 1980 when he was a member of The First Baptist Church in Washington, D.C. and for four years taught a large Sunday School class of young adults. At least half of the members were gay and lesbian. The class included the son and daughter-in-law of President and Mrs. Jimmy Carter. Here was a group of dedicated young adults, homosexual and straight, who were supporting each other while trying to live out their Christian commitment.

In 1980, the author moved to Saint Augustine's parish in southwest Washington, where he was introduced into the Episcopal Church. That first experience as an Episcopalian was exhilarating. The parish membership was comprised of African-Americans and European-Americans, it housed a Jewish temple, and it included a significant number of gay and lesbian persons. The entire congregation, for example, joined in genuine celebration when a lesbian couple adopted a baby.

During the 1990's the Rt. Reverend Ronald Haines served as bishop of the Diocese of Washington. Bishop Haines' son identified himself as gay. This led our bishop through a time of deep struggle. In the end he gave support to his son, to the gay and lesbian clergy in our diocese, and to the civil rights of homosexual persons. During that time people of the diocese had intense debates at many levels. The writer, as a warden, joined all other wardens in the diocese for a two-day conference and dialogue on homosexuality. With the testimony of our bishop and the help of facilitators we moved through the process and agreed to support the inclusion of such persons at every level of church life.

When the writer asks himself what forces influenced his thinking on this subject, he includes his theological education, his prior involvement with the movement for racial justice, and his involvement in efforts to support women's ordination to the priesthood. But what he treasures most are those personal experiences of knowing and working with gay and lesbian persons. A fond hope is that many others in the Church can have similar sacred experiences.

In conclusion, being a responsible pastor or lay leader in a diverse parish is hard work. In urban settings and in areas of large openly gay and lesbian communities, the task of accepting such diversity is much easier. In the northern part of the vast land of China there lies the Great Wall which stretches from east to west through the mountains. Accept the challenge to go for a walk on the Great Wall. The guide will say you have a choice of which direction to take. "There is the very hard climb, and there is the harder climb." The description is apt in deciding how to approach homosexuality in the parish. There are no easy ways. But there are strategies one can devise in being faithful. The parish leader must choose a path as faithful servant of Christ.

Chapter 4
JUSTICE TRANSCENDS TRADITION

> He has told you, O mortal, what is good,
> and what does the Lord require of you but to
> do justice, and to love kindness, and to walk
> humbly with your God.
> —Micah 6:8

> "…with liberty and justice for all."
> —Pledge of Allegiance

A contemporary American irony is that people who demand gestures of patriotism such as requiring school children to repeat the words "…under God, with liberty and justice for all" also lead movements to further write discrimination and injustice into the laws of the land. Yet in the not too distant past we too needed to heed Jesus' words when he said, "You blind guides! You strain at a gnat and swallow a camel."[11]

In 1975 Episcopalians joined other denominations in the National Council of Churches to study the way gays were discriminated against in the workplace. Men known to be gay were denied jobs or were passed over for promotion. The report on the study called for an end to discrimination and equal pay for equal work. The secular press, however, pointed to a glaring inconsistency. Gay men were denied employment in those same churches. Not only was the church pew the most racially segregated place on Sunday morning, but the church also systematically discriminated against lesbians and gays. That beam in the church's eye is just now being removed, freeing us to be honest in the pursuit of justice in the secular workplace.

THE ROLE OF THE CHURCH IN CIVIL SOCIETY

The Church has always had the role of challenging civil society to enact and enforce laws that provide justice for all. However, we dissent on any suggestion that the role of the Church is to control civil society. Jesus never taught a doctrine of domination. Quite the contrary, our Master appeared as "the servant of all." As servant, churches serve civil society by sending forth citizens who promote justice and peace, rather than power or preferment. As servant, churches encourage their members to support candidates for public office whose legislative agenda protects the vulnerable and the rejected while seeking liberty and justice for all. Power, the true church teaches, is not to be hoarded by the few but shared with the many.

We share political power now with other Christians who have a perspective different from ours on many cultural issues. We welcome the debate over homosexuality while we decry all suggestions that our opponents represent the only true voice of Christianity. We accept the challenge to contend in the court of public opinion and in the halls of Congress. We reject the politics of homosexuality that creates prejudice and hysteria. We bring our values of liberty and justice for all and our inherent respect for the dignity and worth of every person, including gays and lesbians.

During the long debate within the Episcopal Church over homosexuality we confess to times of misunderstanding and intolerance. We now hold in our minds a precious image of the Church at General Convention when bishops and deputies were centered and prayerful as they debated and decided in favor of homosexual persons. It is in this pose that we provide a positive role model to the nation.

MASS HYSTERIA AND VIOLENCE

This positive, respectful approach is in contrast to mass hysteria, which has been fanned to a white heat in the culture war over homosexuality. To illustrate, in Virginia a group of students in the Harrisonburg High School came together to support some harassed gay and lesbian classmates with the goal of demonstrating tolerance for each other. They named their organization the "Gay-Straight Alliance." But there were people in town who believed that tolerating homosexuality is the same as promoting it. The issue of permitting this "club" to exist in a high school made its way to the Virginia Senate. At a Senate hearing, persons against homosexuality testified that the club was undermining the sanctity of marriage. In that spirit, Delegate Glenn W. Weatherholz (R-Rockingham) sponsored legislation to forbid what he termed "sex clubs" in the high schools of the state. Soon a political action committee formed to survey attitudes in Virginia. Twenty two thousand people were asked to give a "yes" or "no" answer to the blatantly misleading question, "Do you support sex clubs in our high schools?"

Hysteria goes hand-in-glove with violence against

lesbians and gays. Such incidents are easy to find when one reads carefully the brief stories in the daily newspaper. For example, a 15-year-old girl was standing on a street corner in Newark, New Jersey with friends, waiting for a bus. Two young men drove up and invited the girl to go with them to a party. She declined, saying she was a lesbian. The young men became angry and accused her of being a "dyke." When she resisted them one of the men stabbed her and she died shortly afterward. At his trial the man contended that he did not stab her, but rather, she ran into his knife. The jury reduced the charge from life in prison to 20 to 25 years. The article concluded that lesbians and gays in Newark believe the sentence was reduced because she was a lesbian. Her death has galvanized young lesbians in Newark.[12]

The gay and lesbian community in Washington, D.C. demanded a "Gay and Lesbian Liaison Unit" on the police force. This resulted from police records of 2001 that showed that five transgender persons had been murdered in prison over a period of 14 months. Since the Unit's formation, many gay hate crimes have come to light. The Gay and Lesbian Liaison Unit also does police training for fellow officers so they can learn to treat homosexual persons fairly. To illustrate, a gay man called the police hot line and asked that officers come to his residence at once because he was being abused by his partner. When two officers arrived, rather than try to determine the circumstances or who was at fault, one cop said to the other, "Lock both their gay asses up."[13] These newspaper stories provide glimpses into the world of hysteria, violence and indiscriminate mistreatment of gay and lesbian persons. It happens countless times on a daily basis. Most gay and lesbian persons can testify to slights, slurs and threats to which they are regularly subjected.

TRANSGENDER INJUSTICE

Transgender injustice should be a big issue but it is seldom addressed. Transgender persons may be the most abused and vulnerable group of people in our land. One in every 3,000 babies is born as some type of transgender person, and one in 20,000 babies is born with ambiguous external genitalia. The baby may have a small penis that cannot be distinguished from a large clitoris. However, the laws require that a birth certificate specifying the sex be filled out and recorded, so parents and doctors must choose either male or female. Surgery is often required. For many years most of the medical community assumed that the best procedure was to turn the babies into girls, but this assumption is now being questioned by researchers who follow the development of such children to adulthood. Other transgender persons have bodies not so obviously ambiguous, but whose internal physical characteristics are confusing. Such a person has a complex sexuality. The person may have a very female set of genes in a male body. Or he or she may have a partly formed penis and female breasts. Or the person may be in a woman's body with masculine hair and voice. This individual may or may not be homosexual.

J. Michael Baily has written a splendid book[14] providing case studies of girls who are apparently in boys' bodies. The "boy" at an early age plays with his mother's clothes and wears her high heeled shoes. He plays with pink Barbie dolls and associates with girls at recess but abhors rough sports played by the boys. A famous case was of a boy with the pseudonym "Kraig." His parents desperately wanted their son to be "normal" so they entered him in therapy at age five. His mother was trained to ignore him when he displayed feminine traits. He was "placed on tokens." Kraig was given blue tokens for masculine behavior and red tokens for feminine. His rewards were candy bars and other treats for accumulating blue tokens and he lost television privileges for the "bad" red tokens. According to his therapist, after 60 sessions Kraig engaged in exclusively male-type behavior. However, in the laboratory his team felt that he was acting. At age 17 his mother expressed gratitude for his treatment. He was estranged from his father but he expressed disgust with homosexuality. About this time he had a sexual experience with a gay man in a rest room. Afterward he tried to commit suicide because he believed his parents would be disappointed in him.

Transgender persons are often labeled as "freaks." They once made their livings with traveling circuses, where people paid to enter sideshows and view their non-conformity. Although the sideshows are mostly gone, the alienation and ungodly treatment continues. Such persons deserve our compassion and support as they sort out the most basic issue of their sexuality. A growing number of transsexual persons have surgery to change their physical identity so as to better conform to their sexual perceptions of themselves. We can no longer dismiss this struggle for identity as something evil. Church and society for too long have labeled transgender persons as grossly immoral. A Vatican declaration, for example, stated that transgender persons suffer from mental pathologies and lack moral clarity and hence are barred from serving as

Roman Catholic priests, nuns, monks, friars or brothers in religious orders.

A contemporary Holiness Church in northern Virginia has two members who were transgender. The man knew he was a woman and the woman felt she was a man. After each had surgery they married and were received in church as persons of the opposite gender. Such is the work of the Holy Spirit moving among his people!

This is the conclusion of the Rev. Dr. Justin Tanis, a graduate of Harvard Divinity School. He wrote, "We have learned that our world is far more diverse than we previously imagined and that includes our chromosomal, physical and emotional diversities. This diversity is a part of God's plan and is to be celebrated."[15]

JUSTICE TRANSCENDS TRADITION

What restrictions should the state place on sexual activity? We affirm the right of consenting adults to choose their partners. At what point then should society enforce sexual regulation? We should enact laws to prevent the powerful from exploiting the weak. Society should intervene when sexual activity produces negative societal consequences that clearly impact the public good. From the perspective of justice, however, we should be aware that the regulation of sex is an expression of power. Whether marriage is permitted for same-gender persons is a power decision made by some who control the destiny of others. This is an awesome responsibility. At some point we stop and ask, "Is this power being used fairly?"

Well-meaning persons who oppose inclusion of gays and lesbians as fit for equal treatment in church and society often argue from tradition. They make the case that historically homosexual persons have been deemed immoral and hence rejected by society. Their claim is correct in the sense that most often lesbian and gay persons have been rejected and at many times persecuted, condemned and killed. Again, the term "faggot," used pejoratively to belittle homosexual persons, is taken from the time when such persons were burned at the stake.

For Christians, justice trumps tradition. The history of our country since its birth is the story of one segment of society after another struggling to gain justice by entering the arena of power. It is the dramatic march from unjust traditional patterns of social arrangement to the justice of inclusion. Almost always our Church stood with those who limited the power of all but a few select and privileged people. However, always within the Church the hearts of some Christians were enlightened by the teachings of Jesus. First, a small minority would speak out and stand on the side of the dispossessed. A growing awareness followed as people of conscience realized that the old pattern did not meet the test of fairness. Finally a paradigm shift would emerge, a rearrangement of the basic pattern between the group in question and the governing power. At each point traditionalists believed morality was breaking down, while those who saw the issue as one of justice felt the moral bonds were being strengthened.

At the time of the Continental Congress it was primarily males who were accorded the franchise. Persons with little or no property were usually excluded. Thomas Jefferson led the movement to bring small stakeholders on the frontier into the democratic process of voting and electing persons to represent them.

All African-Americans were excluded by definition. The Dred Scott decision by the Supreme Court, in what many call the most infamous case in Court history, ruled in 1857 that slaves and free Africans could never become citizens and hence could not sue in federal court. Only after the protracted bloody Civil War were slaves freed and declared to be full citizens. The struggle for voting rights went on for another century. Dr. Martin Luther King Jr. likened the small black child entering an all-white school to the children of Israel entering the Promised Land. God heard their cry and said, "Let my people go." His appeal was to the conscience of white oppressors, who, nonetheless, were imbued with latent Christian beliefs.

Few of us in today's church would argue the case for slavery or for the repression of African Americans. But most eighteenth and nineteenth century Christians did. Social conditions changed, prophetic voices spoke and the injustice which marked the old system became evident. In each such crisis the Episcopal Church in General Convention read scripture again, as if for the first time, in the new light of God's love for all persons, and God's demand for justice. A new paradigm was required. Each crisis was a struggle between the old outmoded law and the new law of love, which was more humane. In each crisis justice eventually trumped tradition.

The same pattern was repeated with regard to basic rights for women. Women lacked the franchise, and hence the power to protect themselves or legally advance their interests. The right to vote came in 1920 after a long struggle by the suffrage movement. It took another 60 years for our Church to take down the barriers and

admit women to the priesthood and later to the position
of bishop. The Church experienced a joyous renewal when
the other half of our membership became leaders. Men
finally recognized the injustice long perpetuated against
women, but not until many of these women organized
within church and society in a movement that made their
demands felt.

THE MODERN GAY RIGHTS MOVEMENT

Lesbians and gays have the right to vote, so in that
respect the analogy is not parallel. However, there are
legal and social prohibitions which do parallel those that
existed in these other movements for justice. When this
minority finally organized to gain legal rights, some
of us saw it as a sign of the kingdom, an appropriate
use of power in the service of justice. Justice will be
consummated only when we join the gay and lesbian
community to repeal discriminatory laws, to demand
their protection from vigilantes, and to accord them full
respect.

Gays and lesbians are banding together. Gay marches
proclaim sexual pride. Signs of courage are in evidence
as more persons with hidden identity "come out" and
put their lives on the line by joining the movement. By
banding together and developing a strategy for success,
the gay-lesbian community has emerged as a broad-based
social reform movement in the tradition of the civil rights
struggle.

In its early days the gay rights movement practiced
"the politics of protection," a defensive strategy designed
to protect private lives from public intrusion. Their public
policy goal was to eradicate sodomy laws which made

it a crime for consenting adults to enter same-gender relationships. As late as the 1970's virtually every state had sodomy laws, although state prosecutors seldom enforced them. Nonetheless, the threat hung over them and its stigma was psychologically overwhelming.

In the 1986 Supreme Court case of Bowers vs. Hardwick, Justice White wrote the majority opinion which stated that Georgia could prosecute individuals for engaging in consensual homosexual activity. Justice Lewis Powell considered the issue as trivial and cast the deciding vote in the five to four decision. Powell told one of his clerks that the issue was overblown, as he had never met a gay person in his life. According to Powell's biographer, the clerk to whom he spoke was gay.[16]

The lesbian and gay community developed a public relations program. They also formed organizations to lobby and they campaigned to elect candidates for public office who supported their agenda. They have had considerable success. By June of 2003, 35 states and the District of Columbia had repealed their sodomy laws or had publicly announced that they would not be enforced. But as of that date 11 states still retained them. Attorneys again took a case to the Supreme Court of the United States and in a landmark decision the court ruled that all sodomy laws are unconstitutional.

Once decriminalization was achieved in law, the gay rights movement turned its attention to laws that discriminate against homosexual persons. Progress has been steady. Laws have been enacted making it illegal to deny jobs, housing, credit or public accommodations based on sexual orientation. Yet opposition to such laws can only be described as fierce, and the movement recognizes that the gains could easily turn to losses. Many laws and public policies remain outdated. For example, on May 24, 2005, a U.S. Senate panel met to ensure that federal employees and contractors were enforcing the discrimination laws aimed at fairness. The question before the panel was whether federal employers can legally discriminate against employees, based on sexual orientation. Special Counsel Scott J. Bloch told the committee that the courts had rejected sexual orientation as a protected class. Mr. Bloch claimed, therefore, that he had no authority to bring charges against federal agencies when they discriminated against lesbians and gays. The panel pointed out that the White House had issued a statement in April 2004 saying its position was to protect gays and lesbians in the federal workplace. The White House statement concluded, "President Bush expects federal agencies to enforce this policy and to ensure that all federal employees are protected from unfair discrimination at work." Nevertheless, Mr. Bloch declared that he could not enforce this policy. Why? "Because," he said, "I am limited by the enforcement statutes that you give me. Legally, sexual orientation is not included along with race, religion, sex, age, national origin, disability and political affiliation."[17]

Representative Barney Frank, an openly gay Congressman from Massachusetts, introduced legislation in July 2005 to allow gay or lesbian spouses of employees of the federal government to qualify for health insurance, retirement and other benefits. The Congressman made the case that private enterprise is far ahead of government agencies in granting these provisions for same-gender couples. Mr. Frank pointed out that more than 8,000 employers across the country provide domestic partner benefits. In addition, he estimated that more than 200 of the Fortune 500 companies and 150 state and local government entities offer benefits to same-gender partners. The House Bill defines a domestic partner as an adult living with, but not married to, another adult "in a committed, intimate relationship."[18]

The nation's law schools have taken their stand for justice. The Association of American Law Schools excludes from membership any school that refuses to ban a law firm from recruiting on its campus if that firm does not agree to give equal consideration to persons who are openly gay or lesbian. The prospective law firm's recruiter must "observe the principle of equal opportunity."

The author serves on the Advisory Social Services Board for Fairfax County, Virginia, a county with a million people. We have protective oversight for children who are orphans, for children who are abused in their homes, or where parental care is grossly inadequate. The staff is searching constantly for foster and adoptive parents. Many children would be blessed if they could be placed in loving, stable homes of same-gender couples. Yet in Virginia this has become impossible based on a recently enacted state law forbidding such placement. This becomes a justice issue both for children needing stable homes and for same-gender couples seeking the opportunity to serve these children.

MARRIAGE AS A JUSTICE ISSUE

The next step in the long march toward equality in the gay rights movement impacts our churches more directly. Lesbians and gays are now focusing their efforts on obtaining the right to marry. They demand that the state as a matter of justice provide them the right to a civil union. They ask for the civil protections and state-given benefits taken for granted by heterosexual couples. For example, they seek the right to jointly own property. Lesbians and gays want the ability to pass their assets to their legal partners at death. They ask the right to claim health insurance benefits when a partner can no longer work. They want the right to visit their committed partner in the hospital during a health crisis, and they want to participate in decisions for the terminally ill. These and dozens of other civil "rights" are legally denied to them in many states and would be rectified through civil marriage.

The gay rights movement is now having a lively internal debate over strategy. Some want to press for full acceptance which they see as marriage rather than civil union. The issue is whether it is politically more practical to seek half a loaf and settle for unions. Those who take this side argue that there is little importance to whether the name is union or marriage so long as the civil rights and legal protections are afforded to them as citizens. Others contend that the term "union" has a stigma that signifies their status is lower than those who are married.

Churches will decide whether gays and lesbians can be married, united or neither in a Christian ceremony. This is appropriate because only our churches can define Christian marriage and freely bless this sacred rite. Permanent unions as civil contracts will satisfy a large portion of the gay and lesbian community since the church has little, if any, place in their lives. The issue is quite different for those who are Christian and who desire marriage with the blessing of God. The resolution is a justice issue for Christians.

A strong case can be made for a universal right to civil unions. Good citizens believe in stable families. As public health advocates we want to limit the spread of the deadly AIDS virus. As human beings we affirm the need for intimacy with its potential for love and joy. Justice calls us to make available to gay and lesbian persons the same rights to stability, health and love that are afforded to heterosexual couples. Certainly the legal protections and benefits of marriage should be extended to same-gender couples.

It is hard for some of us who find our intimacy and sexual fulfillment with a person of the other gender to imagine compatibility with a person of the same gender. For many of us the thought is abhorrent. Yet the consistent testimony of gay and lesbian persons is that for them same-gender marriage is the path to fulfillment. It is a denial of their personhood to enter life-long marriage with a person of the opposite gender.

THE CAPACITY TO EMPATHIZE

For us to pursue justice we need the capacity to empathize with the victim. We feel deep within ourselves the actual experience of injustice, as if the slap were in our faces. As Christians, we are invited to walk in the sandals of One unjustly treated. We take up the cross as we feel the pain of the other and stand in solidarity with the oppressed. Every heterosexual Christian who has been blessed by a strong marriage and a loving family should have the capacity to empathize with those for whom this "right" is denied.

The justice process lets us hear the voices of the oppressed. We struggle to connect the dots as we more fully understand the injustices faced by homosexual persons. But there is a final step. We want to "do" justice. Doing justice requires our ongoing support. We hear the God of justice calling us to action in a partnership with those unfairly treated. We join hands and hearts in praying that the "shalom" of God may be realized within their community, between their aspirations and our own, and in all corners of an unfair world.

THE UNTHINKABLE IS UNDENIABLE

The unthinkable is now undeniable. Our blind eyes are opening to a great injustice. The Episcopal Church in the United States recognizes by its very nature that it has a role in standing with homosexual persons as both priest and prophet. Priests serve as mediators, as pastors, bringing the congregation where all are welcome into fellowship with each other. Prophets repeat the ancient message, "Thus says the Lord" as justice is proclaimed and new paradigms are forged. Clergy have the awesome task of finding ways to speak the word of God even when the message is unpopular and difficult for some parishioners to hear.

As priests and leaders of the Church we do not want to stretch the bonds of fellowship or break the harmony of shared mission. Today's prophet has genuine love for the entire Church and speaks only because God's heart is broken by injustice toward others of God's children. We affirm that the very heartbeat of God requires justice even while we recognize that good people find reason to inadvertently stand on the side of injustice.

Some still dispute the claim that gay and lesbian persons are victims of injustice. They claim that homosexual persons generally get what they deserve. When the state withholds rights granted to heterosexuals, when they are excluded from employment opportunities, or when they are required to suppress their identities in the armed forces, these persons claim they are only protecting the innocent. Those who dispute the claim of injustice assume that gays and lesbians are practicing sinners who need only turn from their wicked ways. They can be accepted as good citizens in church or society if they will but repent, amend their lives by overcoming their same-sex obsessions and begin living as God intended.

Those who believe that sexual orientation for most persons is a given and not a choice find the injustice to be profound. We believe that when God made some people with same-gender orientation, God made them good like the rest of us. Why, we ask, should people be punished for the way God made them? As one lay theologian remarked, "God don't make junk."

Chapter 5
THE WITNESS OF SCRIPTURE

> "All scripture is inspired by God and is useful
> for teaching, for reproof, for correction and for
> training in righteousness."
> —II Timothy 3:16

> "But avoid stupid controversies...and quarrels
> about the law; for they are unprofitable and
> worthless."
> —Titus 3:9

The Episcopal Church in the United States shares
with other branches of the Anglican Communion and
with other historic churches that comprise mainline
Christianity the belief that Holy Scripture is authoritative
for our lives. As stated in Article VI in the Articles of
Religion, published in 1801, "Holy Scripture containeth
all things necessary to salvation...." Every priest of the
Episcopal Church affirms this article as a prerequisite to
ordination.

Most of us in the Episcopal Church believe that the
Bible is the source for our faith and doctrine, but that
it is not inerrant. The Bible was not written by a divine
hand, in such a way that every word contains absolute
truth. A better way to state our understanding is to say
the Bible contains the Word of God. The Bible contains
the dramatic story of God creating the world and human
life, of the willful fall from innocence of the human race

into wayward and sinful rebellion against God. It contains the story of a covenant made between God and the people of Israel. As part of that covenant came the law by which Israel would seek to live so as to honor God. The Bible is the story of God reaching out in love to rescue humankind from sin and death. In the New Testament Gospels we rejoice to find the life and teachings of Jesus that reveal the law of love as the new way to approach life. This Bible story culminates in a new covenant (testament) made by Jesus the Christ for the redemption of the world. We affirm that the Jesus story must always be the norm for our faith and practice.

Whatever our conclusion might be about the acceptance of gay and lesbian persons in society and in church, we all agree that it should be centered in our best understanding of scripture. We shall study in detail all same-gender sexual references found in the Bible. Our purpose is to look at the texts honestly. To achieve this goal we must also consider the historical and cultural settings for the exegesis. Some object to this larger study, accusing us of "tampering" with the plain text. Those of us who insist on the necessity of this process believe it to be essential if we are to discern the "story behind the headlines."

OLD TESTAMENT PASSAGES
Genesis 19:1-11

This is the story of Lot, a nephew of Abraham, who had moved to the sophisticated city of Sodom when his herds grew too large for the available grass in the area where Abraham was living. Lot was an alien, living in an urban culture, far from his Hebrew clan.

A righteous man in this early Hebrew culture always offered hospitality to strangers. So, when two travelers appeared at the city gates, Lot offered to let the men stay at his home. But some men of Sodom who did not appreciate having a foreigner living among them were especially angry that Lot showed hospitality for other alien visitors. So the men of Sodom conspired to humiliate the aliens in the most violent way they could imagine. Not only would the strangers be abused physically, they would also be humiliated by treating them like women, thus emasculating them.

While Lot was dining with the visitors, who were really angels, men of the city came to his house and shouted for Lot to bring the visitors outside. They announced their plan to gang rape the men. Lot gave supreme importance to hospitality and so he decided to protect the men at any cost. He went out and offered the rabble his two virgin daughters, and said to them, "...do to them as you please."[19]

Fortunately the strangers helped Lot get back inside the house, and before the daughters could be rounded up, the angels blinded the men outside. The next day Lot and his wife escaped the city at the direction of the angels, who announced that God planned to destroy the city because of its evil. We remember how Lot's wife looked back after the couple had been warned against doing so. She was turned into a pillar of salt, as sulfur and fire from heaven rained down on Sodom, and another wicked city, Gomorrah.[20]

In summary, the story as told countless times in Hebrew history depicts Sodom as an evil city for rejecting hospitality to strangers, while Lot is seen as an example of gracious hospitality. It also condemns homosexual gang rape. This brutal behavior has nothing to do with whether we should affirm same-gender couples who mutually love each other.

Judges 19:16-30

This story is similar to the one in Genesis leading to the destruction of Sodom. A traveler with his family was returning from Bethlehem to his home in the hill country of Ephraim. He stopped for the night at Gibeah and asked for lodging at the home of an old man, after others had turned him away. The old man welcomed the travelers, fed the donkeys, washed the feet of the weary travelers, and gave them dinner.

But some men of the town, "a perverse lot" came to the house, demanding that the male traveler come outside, "...so that we may have intercourse with him."[21] The host pleaded with them to go away, but then to appease them, he offered his virgin daughter and the concubine of the visitor. Then the visitor seized his concubine and took her outside and told the men to ravish her. "They wantonly raped her and abused her all through the night until morning."[22]

The next morning the master of the house found the concubine at his doorstep, dazed and unable to speak. The visitor put her on a donkey and set out for home. The story implies that the young woman died on the journey. The visitor then took a knife and cut her body into twelve pieces, limb by limb, and sent her remains throughout the territory of Israel to show the kind of evil men who lived in Gibeah.

We can appreciate the hospitality the old man

showed for his visitors, and we believe he was right to reject the gang rape of a visitor. We can assume that he felt it necessary to offer the young woman to appease the men. The story gives us a glimpse into the reality of Hebrew society where men held concubines whose lives were of lesser value. The moral sensibilities of that culture do not resonate with our own. Again, this passage does not deal directly with the question of consenting homosexuality, but only the issues of hospitality and brutal gang rape.

Leviticus: 18:1-5, 22; 20:13

In these passages we move away from stories of gang rape to consider Jewish law that deals directly with homosexual acts. Two verses clearly state the law: "You shall not lie with a male as with a woman. It is an abomination."[23] "If a man lies with a male as with a woman, both of them have committed an abomination; they shall be put to death, their blood is upon them."[24]

Dr. Ellen F. Davis, Associate Professor of Old Testament Language and Literature at Virginia Theological Seminary, wrote a helpful article on how to read Leviticus in church. She suggested that the early New Testament Church struggled with the same issue of what constitutes holiness, much as we do, as they read about holiness in Leviticus. As a tribal people the Hebrews were offended by Canaanite sexual practices such as temple prostitution. Our problem is how to apply this text so as to make it meaningful for our situation. Dr. Davis suggests that the clergy has an unfinished task in helping the laity understand how to proceed.[25]

These laws are identified with Moses, the original

law-giver. As told in the first passage, the people are to obey their God and not become involved in immoral practices of the Canaanites.[26] A series of forbidden practices follows. The first verses forbid nudity of any woman, "uncovering nakedness." Then we find the prohibition against uncovering the nakedness of even a married woman during her menstrual period, essentially forbidding sexual intercourse then between married persons. Next Israel's men were forbidden to have sexual relations with "your kinsman's wife."[27] Finally, just prior to the verse on same-gender prohibition is one that forbade sacrificing the life of a Hebrew child to Molech.

Some scholars divide Hebrew laws into two categories. Secondary offenses, while severe, fell into the category that included eating unclean food such as shellfish, pork and other meat from hoofed animals, or touching a dead person, or a man having sexual intercourse with his wife during her menstrual period. Primary offenses deserving death included sexual sins, such as a man having intercourse with another man's wife. These death sentences also fell on homosexuality, incest, and bestiality. Other scholars do not discern a notable difference in Hebrew thought between primary and secondary laws, in that people were required to obey all of them. Same-gender sexual relations were among the worst and were considered to be an "abomination" punishable by death. The question is, "Why?"

From a study of Hebrew culture one can discern several reasons:

- Hebrew pre-scientific biology taught that male semen contained the "life force," with no knowledge of the importance of female eggs and ovulation. It was assumed that the woman merely provided the incubation space. Hence, the spilling of semen was considered immoral, whether by male masturbation or male homosexual acts.

- In an era when Hebrew tribes were surrounded by hostile aliens, every person was important and maximum procreation was obligatory. The command to "multiply" was understood as important to tribal self-preservation, and to Israel's power in the geo-political struggles. Homosexual unions would not contribute to the drive for domination.

- When a man assumed the role of a woman sexually, male dignity and dominance were compromised. Sexual acts in tribal society were much less about mutual love and a great deal more about power relationships. Homosexual behavior was, therefore, a threat to male domination in the social structure of the tribe. Scholars have noted that there were no similar laws prohibiting lesbianism.

- Hebrews, as a people of the covenant, wanted to separate themselves from surrounding cultures and obtain a level of purity that would make them distinctive. They wanted to present themselves holy, acceptable unto God. The entire package of dietary and sexual prohibitions was an honest desire for holiness.

- Finally, there was concern among lawgivers to maintain neat categories and a sense of orderliness in all aspects of the common life.

"You shall not let your animals breed with a different kind; you shall not sow your field with two kinds of seed; nor shall you put on a garment made of two different materials."[28] Similarly, a woman who wears a man's clothing commits an abomination.[29] Likewise, acts of homosexual conduct were considered mixing the order of creation in opposition to nature, as established by God.

These considerations lead us to conclude that homosexuality was forbidden, not because of a moral absolute, but rather the prohibition was based on local mores, faulty physiological analysis, a male dominated culture, competition with surrounding tribes and a genuine desire to achieve holiness before God. The concept of mutuality and integrity for persons genetically created with same-gender orientation was never considered and therefore no conclusions were ever reached on that topic. Yes, homosexuality was condemned, but the reasons were relative and local, not universal and eternal.

For God's people in the time of the Hebrew Bible, these laws were not arbitrary but were of grave importance. The issue is whether they were expressions of an evolving ethic, accepted for their time and place, but not relevant for us. Or, was theirs a "normative ethic," one that was absolute and universal for all times. Would we not agree that it was the former? Let us explore a bit further.

There were many other sins of the Hebrews that also deserved the death penalty. "If you have a stubborn or rebellious son who will not obey his father and mother, then bring him to the elders. All of the men in the town shall stone him to death, so you shall purge the evil from your midst."[30]

Note that the Law condoned slavery and polygamy. In war, if a warrior of Israel came across a beautiful woman whom he desired, the law permitted him to capture her. However, when he brought her to his house he should marry her, but only after he had let her mourn for a month for her father and mother. "But if you later are not satisfied with her, you shall let her go free and not sell her for money...You must not treat her as a slave, since you have dishonored her."[31]

These are harsh laws, tinged with humanism. They reflect a culture with mores that are not appropriate for us in this modern era. Rather than assume a divine inerrancy in the reading of particular scripture verses and then accept these laws as literal words from God for us to follow, a more promising approach is to accept them as tribal customs, provided by lawgivers in the form of judges, and later priests, for the people of that era.

We note in passing that many of these tribal customs that seem so abhorrent to us now are still being practiced among some Muslim fundamentalists, who take these passages literally. Hence, in Sudan, tribal warriors capture Christian women and children and sell them into slavery or take them as personal slaves. Women found in adultery are still stoned to death in Afghanistan. A literal acceptance of Hebrew Scripture can lead to brutal consequences. We recognize that it is easy to misconstrue scripture by reading it literally, and thus do great harm in the name of religion.

We should not make light of the severe

condemnation of homosexuality in Hebrew culture. But neither should we make tribal law, with all of its brutality and failings, into an absolute criterion for judging responsible same-gender marriage in our day.

Positively, God was at work among the lawgivers of Israel as God called them to a more humane society. This better social order was commanded by a God of love and by the demands of justice. Their lifestyle included radical hospitality to strangers. It called for leaving some grain in the field at harvest so the poor could provide for their needs. The Law called for giving alms to the poor and lending without interest on the money. And there was provision for the year of Jubilee, when wealth of the land was re-divided among the people, so that rich and poor could start over on a more level playing field. The Law, in short, had within it the seeds of a way of life where the love of neighbor as oneself could blossom and grow into a reality.

The overarching purpose of these laws was to create a holy people, acceptable to a holy God. Israel is called to a life of purity, despite the idolatry of the surrounding cultures. Finally, the law points to the love ethic adopted by Jesus. We note that the command to "Love your neighbor as yourself"[32] is located between the two statements of the law on homosexual conduct found in Leviticus 18 and 20.

Other Old Testament References To Homosexuality

The other references are comments on the sinful lifestyle of Sodom and hence God's punishment of the city.[33] There is no specific comment on homosexuality, only the widespread sin of Sodom, and a call for the people of Israel to turn from their wicked ways. In Ezekiel, the sins of Sodom are pride, gluttony, and indifference to the needy. One concludes from these references that the Bible did not assert that the sin of Sodom was homosexuality.

SAYINGS OF JESUS

Jesus did not speak directly to the issue of homosexuality. We wish he had revealed how he viewed this subject, but as on so many topics of great concern to the Church in our day, Jesus appears to have been silent.

He did comment on Sodom's sin, but this was in the context of hospitality for the disciples and it spoke to the sin of inhospitality. "But whenever you enter a town and they do not welcome you; go out into the streets and say, 'Even the dust of your town that clings to our feet, we wipe off in protest against you.' You know this: The Kingdom of God has come near. I tell you on that day it will be more tolerable for Sodom than for that town."[34] One can speculate that if Jesus were concerned with homosexuality as sinful this would have been a good place to say so, since he spoke of the sin of Sodom.

In describing the time of judgment at the end of the age, Jesus likened the coming destruction to that of Sodom. "Likewise, just as it was in the days of Lot: they were eating and drinking, buying and selling, planting and building, but on the day that Lot left Sodom, it rained fire and sulfur from heaven and destroyed all of them—it will be like that on the day that the Son of Man is revealed."[35]

Finally, there is an intriguing account of healing that many scholars believe had same-gender sexual overtones. At Capernaum a centurion came to Jesus and appealed to him saying, "Lord, my servant is lying at home paralyzed, in terrible distress." Jesus offered to come with the soldier and cure the servant. But the centurion demurred, saying he was not worthy to have Jesus come to his house. He noted his own great power to get things done according to his wishes. "...and to my slave, 'Do this,' and the slave does it.'" He suggested that Jesus could heal the man without going to his house. The story ends with the statement that the servant was healed that very hour.[36]

What could justify the conclusion that the slave had a homoerotic relationship with his master? We know from historic sources that such relationships were common in Roman society and were accepted as quite normal, so long as the men were not from the same social class. Living as Jesus did in Galilee, where Roman presence and influence were strong, he was probably aware of the Roman practice of sex slaves across class lines. Matthew used the Greek word for servant or slave that has sexual overtones. In the third century when Jerome translated the gospels into Latin he used the word *puer* to translate from the Greek, thus maintaining the sexual intent in the word. If this interpretation is correct the words of Jesus commending the Roman soldier for his faith, greater than that of any person of Israel, have added meaning.[37] His actions spoke louder than words, as they did in accepting tax collectors, prostitutes and Samaritans.

OTHER NEW TESTAMENT REFERENCES
Romans 1:26-27

A context is needed to understand this primary passage in which the Apostle Paul mentions homosexuality. The Epistle to the Romans was written from Corinth prior to Paul's first visit to the capital city. He knew the church was composed rather equally of Jew and Gentile Christians, and that they were not getting along. Rather than side with one party over the other, Paul used this letter as a theological argument for shared community life. His message was for each to respect the other, since both sides included wrongdoers.

Comments by Paul in the first chapter of Romans offer the most significant passage in the New Testament that addresses homosexuality. The whole passage is a powerful attack on Gentile idolatry. Paul lays out a long list of evil practices he has observed in Gentile culture. In chapter two he turns the tables and says he finds equally troublesome practices among the Jews. They are similar in the sense that they are equally offensive to God. Therefore, he warned, neither Jews nor Gentiles should pass judgment against the other. Especially the Jews have "no excuse" for passing judgment on others.[38] Paul then drew the powerful conclusion, "All have sinned and fall short of the glory of God." [39] But all have the same means of salvation: "...he justifies the one who has faith in Jesus."[40]

What Paul is doing within the larger purpose of the letter is showing the sin of all humanity before the perfect justice of God. He is therefore explaining the logical wrath of God against all humanity. He then makes a complete turn and shows that the righteousness of God has been revealed in the death and resurrection of Christ and that God justifies those who believe the gospel.

With this larger context in mind, we return to chapter one and the statement on homosexual practice. Paul states that idolatry results when we suppress the truth of God that lies deep within us all. There is an option for us: either we choose the path of wisdom, of worshipping and serving our creator, or we choose the foolish path. The fruit of idolatry is all manner of evil, both sins of the flesh and sins of the spirit. "God gave them up in the lusts of their hearts." He then gives one example of degrading physical passion, followed by twenty-one examples of the debased mind.

"Their women exchanged natural intercourse for unnatural, and in the same way also the men, giving up natural intercourse with women, were consumed with passion for one another. Men committed shameless acts with men and received in their own persons the due penalty for their error."[41]

In Hellenistic Jewish literature a common criticism of Greeks was their same-gender sexual proclivity. Among the relationships that were the most despicable was pederasty, an ongoing relationship between a mature man and a boy, in which the man assumed the active role. Another common societal practice, as described in the healing by Jesus, was for a military officer or a person of elevated social status to "keep" a partner for homosexual activity. It is worth noting that same-gender sexual activity was seldom reported among men of the same age and social class.

A study guide on marriage, same-sex unions and the Church titled, *An Honorable Estate*, prepared for use in the Episcopal Church in Canada, points out that Paul must have been familiar with the writings of Seneca, Philo, and Dio Chrysostom who were contemporary moralists.[42] These writers spelled out in detail their view that some men seem "supercharged" with sex. Such men grow weary of satisfying their lust with women. They then move on to lust with men and boys, and finally, in the extreme of insatiable lust, turn to animals. Perhaps Paul was expressing that viewpoint when he indicated that homosexuality was based on inordinate desire—heterosexual lust taken to an extreme. We must take seriously this explicit condemnation but at the same time recognize that the circumstance described was very different from the issue we confront of two persons who wish to make a long-term commitment to each other and do so in a morally responsible way. Those familiar with first century moral philosophy believe Paul was talking about immoderate passions of heterosexual persons.

It is evident that Paul was unaware of the distinction between sexual orientation as a "given" versus sexual behavior based on choice. He seems to assume that these Romans were heterosexual persons who were acting contrary to nature, exchanging their "normal" orientation for one that was foreign to them. In other words, Paul thought that he was writing about "straight" people who adopted by choice a gay or lesbian lifestyle. For him, these persons were acting contrary to nature. With our knowledge of homosexuality we can argue they may, in fact, have been acting according to their nature.

Indeed, the modern term "sexual relations" tends to assume mutuality, consent and equality. The Greek word **chresin** used here as "sexual intercourse" does not necessarily imply such mutuality but rather suggests that encounters were exploitive. Paul used the Greek word common in his day and probably had in mind a contrast to his description of love and mutuality described elsewhere in Christian marriage.

The passage in Romans is distinctive in that it is the only place in the Bible that speaks of same-gender sexual activity among women. Paul makes a sweeping claim about "Gentile women" but he does not spell out exactly what he has in mind. Some have suggested that he referred here to women who refused to accept a passive role in marital sexuality. Paul does not say that the females indulged in same-gender activity, but only exchanged what is customary for what is unnatural.

The words that describe female relations are *para physin* or contrary to nature. What did Paul mean by using these words? One school of thought suggests that Paul is referring to the Genesis account of creation of man and woman and their "natural" physical reciprocal relationship. If so, he spoke about lesbian relationships. Other interpreters view these words quite differently. For people of that era, "nature" expressed what is conventional and "unnatural" is a synonym for that which is unconventional. Again, he may have been making reference to unnatural acts of wives who took dominant roles in sexual relations with their husbands. Whatever the specific situation he has in mind, he is discussing the wrath of God against all humanity and is not intending to provide a detailed account of the place of homosexuality. He is also dealing with real-life issues within the church at Rome, whatever they may have been.

I Corinthians 6:9-11

On a different but related matter Paul rebuked the church at Corinth for permitting a man to remain in good standing who was living with his father's wife, presumably his step-mother. Paul admonished the church not to associate with sexually immoral persons.[43] He wrote, "Do you not know that wrongdoers will not inherit the kingdom of God? Do not be deceived! Fornicators, idolaters, adulterers, male prostitutes, sodomites, thieves, the greedy, drunkards, revilers, robbers—none of these will inherit the kingdom of God."

Paul had received reports about divisions within the congregation and questions about how church members should conduct themselves. The letter is an extended plea for unity in the body of Christ. It is, further, Paul's response to questions about sexual immorality in the church at Corinth. The tone of admonition is evident in his first words, "Do you not know?" Paul is telling them what he has told them before. Paul pleads with his congregants not to be deceived. The words can also be translated, "do not go astray." He then lists ten activities that are to be opposed.

Of the ten items, there are three that are of particular interest for our consideration: *pornoi*, *malakoi*, and *arsenokoitai*.

Pornos. This singular form means "one who practices sexual immorality" or "fornicator." The word can be used to refer to a male prostitute but it has a larger connotation and can be applied to a whole range of sexual activities. In one reference Paul writes to a Christian man who has been seeing a prostitute and calls his actions, "immoral." In like fashion he labels the actions of the man living with his stepmother as ***pornos***.

Malakoi and ***arsenokoitai***. These words are more central to our discussion regarding same-gender proclivity. The usual view is that the two words are related. Each term sheds light on the other. The word ***malakoi*** is the word for "soft." The King James Version translates the word, "effeminate." The Revised Standard Version translated the two words taken together as "homosexuals." This was revised in the 1971 version and was translated as "sexual perverts." The word ***malakoi*** was often used to refer to prepubescent boys used in pederasty, and the word ***arsenokoitai*** was used to refer to those who kept them for their sexual favors.

Whatever Paul had in mind, he wrote, "...and this is what some of you used to be."[44] Paul concluded, "Drive out the wicked person from among you."[45] Some biblical literalists use this instruction as a mandate for them to reject homosexual persons and drive them out of the church. Others of us believe that Paul was responding to the exploitation of boys by powerful men.

I Timothy 1:9-10

The final reference in the New Testament is in the first letter of Timothy. "This means understanding that the law is laid down not for the innocent but for the lawless and disobedient, for the godless and sinful, for the unholy and profane, for those who kill their father or mother, for murderers, fornicators, sodomites, slave traders, liars, perjurers, and whatever else is contrary to the sound teaching."

Again there are three words of special interest, two of which we encountered in I Corinthians. They are *pornoi*, *arsenokoitai*, and the new term, *andrapodistai*. The last word is often translated "kidnappers." The term can be defined as "one who procures persons for use by others." On some occasions the word has meant "slave-dealer."

There are two ways one can view these words and thus determine what, if anything, they have to say on our subject. The first approach is to take the words together. There is an active homosexual partner, a passive partner and a hired person who procures the passive partner. There is no sense of an equal partnership in the sexual relationship. Often a child was kidnapped and sold into sexual slavery. This passage simply does not deal with same-gender relationships on a mature and mutual level.

The other way to interpret these terms is to consider them as independent of each other. *Pornoi* has a generic meaning, a general term that refers to sexual activities. The term *andrapodistai* simply means a kidnapper without any reference to prostitution. This leaves *arsenokoitai* which probably means homosexual, although the concept was unknown at that time. For some scholars, the term means one who actively engaged in same-gender sexual relations. But for others the term means persons involved in pederasty. It should be noted that sins denounced in Timothy coincide with the Ten Commandments. These are persons who break the Ten Commandments, and here, specifically, the command against adultery.[46]

REFLECTIONS ON THE BIBLICAL ANALYSIS

Modern Christians cannot in good conscience affirm a significant portion of Old Testament law. Many of these laws are judged to be barbaric and as such deeply offend our sensibilities. Leviticus is a strange mixture of punitive taboo regulations, carefully defined purity regulations, and lofty ethical norms. The issue at hand is to determine in which category the verses on same-gender sexual relations should be placed. Is this prohibition a reflection of descriptive cultural practices or is it a normative ethical standard to be upheld for all times?

The Law was still there in Jesus' day, although the Rabbis had circumscribed it with detailed interpretations and the Proverbs had distilled its common sense meaning. As we shall see in the next chapter, Jesus was quick to set aside the Law. Jesus never addressed the issue of homosexuality. Some argue that Jesus surely accepted the norm of his day, or else he would have spoken clearly on the matter. Others contend that it was not of major importance or he would have addressed the issue. Many New Testament scholars believe that Jesus reached out in compassion and healed the sex partner of the centurion soldier. We must leave the question unanswered as to why Jesus did not speak specifically to it.

Paul wrote directly against certain homosexual practices well known among many Gentile men and women. In addition, he listed twenty-one sins of the spirit. He specifically asked the Jews in the congregation at Rome not to judge Greek culture in a way that would break the harmony of their fellowship in the church. Various interpretations are possible for I Corinthians and Timothy, although it is evident that some forms of

112

homosexuality are regarded as opposed to the nature and will of God.

The Bible writers never consider the possibility of responsible, caring, long-term committed relationships between same-gender persons, to determine whether such unions could produce the fruits of the Spirit. We certainly have evidence that many contemporary gay and lesbian Christians do produce these fruits, contrary to the list of negative qualities in Romans 1. Biblical writers knew nothing of modern conceptions of homosexuality as a condition rather than a choice. Indeed, the word, "homosexual" did not enter the English language until the latter part of the nineteenth century. The earliest entry for the word "homosexual" in an English dictionary was in the 1892 edition of *The Oxford English Dictionary*. One concludes that the Bible writers had no modern conception of homosexuality as a biological given rather than a choice and hence have said nothing about the kind of homosexuality with which we are concerned. It becomes evident after a careful study of all biblical references that the issue cannot be settled by biblical proof-texts.

Jesus proclaimed by word and deed a new law for Christians. His law of love fulfilled ancient Jewish law and gave it new meaning. Every moral problem had to pass the test provided by the law of love. This is the exciting and liberating ethic taught by the Master. We are left until the next chapter with the question of whether the ethic of Jesus would affirm same-gender marriage and full participation in the life of the Church in our day.

Chapter 6
LAW, WISDOM, AND THE LOVE ETHIC OF JESUS

> Just then a lawyer stood up to test Jesus.
> "Teacher," he said, "what must I do to inherit
> eternal life?" He said to him, "What is written
> in the law? What do you read there?" He
> answered, "You shall love the Lord your God
> with all your heart, and with all your soul, and
> with all your strength, and with all your mind;
> and your neighbor as yourself." And he said to
> him, "You have given the right answer. Do this
> and you shall live."
> —Luke 10: 25-28

We begin with the assumption that for Christians what Jesus taught and lived carries greater weight than any other consideration.

The legal structures for Jewish morality in Jesus' day were found in Exodus, Leviticus and Deuteronomy. Jewish tradition provided interpretations as to what each law meant and how it was to be applied. There was a law, for example, related to the Sabbath. Israelites were to do their work for six days and then rest on the seventh. They were to remember the Sabbath day and keep it holy.

By the time the young Jesus burst on the scene of his public ministry there were literally dozens of rules related to what work one could do on the Sabbath. How much could the wife of the household cook? How far could a person walk? Could the donkey be fed? How much? Keeping the Sabbath holy had come to involve a complex set of prescriptions.

JESUS AND THE LAW

The Scribes and Pharisees marveled at what they considered to be Jesus' disrespect for the law and its tradition. Jesus taught on the Sabbath and he and his disciples plucked ears of corn for a meal on the Sabbath.[47] Further, he insisted that it was appropriate to heal an infirm man on the Sabbath. Jesus asked a man with a withered hand to stretch it out. He did so, and his hand was restored. How did those responsible for keeping the law respond? "...they were filled with fury."[48]

Jewish law and tradition required people to wash their hands and say a prayer before eating. Jesus did not do this ritual cleansing. Why would he flout the law and break the traditions built up over hundreds of years? Jesus responded that it is relatively unimportant to cleanse the outside of the cup and the plate, but one's thoughts and speech that come from within are extremely important. Again, "...the Pharisees marveled."[49]

Jesus wanted Israel to keep every law written in the Pentateuch in the sense that the spirit of the law was supremely important.[50] But that was far different from being bound by specific laws, as required by the Pharisees, who considered themselves to be the gatekeepers. Jesus' position seemed odd to people who heard it, because the Pharisees spent hours every day in praying, ritual cleansing, alms giving and keeping other commandments. Indeed, one had to have independent wealth to be a Pharisee because keeping the law was a

116

full-time job. Obviously, the ethic of Jesus differed from that of his contemporaries.

The Essenes were another major sect with whom to contrast the ethic of Jesus. While they are not referred to directly in the gospels, we know about them primarily from the Dead Sea Scrolls. They chose the path of asceticism, living as a sect apart, according to strict community rules. They were very serious about exceeding the righteousness of others in the tradition of Israel. Jesus did not offer the sectarian option as being a better, more serious way to obey the law.

Jesus said each law must stand the test: "You shall love the Lord your God with all of your heart, soul, strength, and mind, and you shall love your neighbor as yourself."[51] This love for God and love for neighbor is the ethic behind all of the particular 613 commandments in the Old Testament. If those 613 laws do not measure up to the law of love in common sense practical ways, the laws should be modified or discarded in favor of doing what love demands in the circumstance.

Obviously then, Jesus' ethic was not a set of rigid "do's and don'ts." His ethic was not found in following some literal inerrant scripture verse from the Hebrew Bible. His powerful message was that of the prophets: do justice and love mercy because a God of love requires this. His ethic was founded on his profound respect for people—all kinds of people—women, children, foreigners, wealthy, lower class, races long ostracized, and prostitutes, among others. His concern was to announce the coming of the kingdom of God, and to invite all people to enter. His wrath was reserved for those who placed roadblocks in the way of those who would like to enter. He called them "blind guides."[52]

JESUS' USE OF THE WISDOM LITERATURE

Let us turn to the use Jesus made of Wisdom Literature.[53] The Hebrew Bible used by Jesus was divided into three categories. First, the Law retained primary importance for regulating the moral life. However, by the time of Jesus, virtually nobody believed that this law alone was sufficient to guide the moral life or direct the courts. Second, the Prophets set a standard for social justice against the pressures of wealth and political power. Third, "The Writings" revealed a tradition of personal morality based on prudence and experience. These writings were among the latest added to the Old Testament and were referred to as Wisdom Literature. Many of the more barbaric rules and early laws no longer seemed appropriate, so the later rabbis encouraged common sense wisdom to replace the extremes of the law.

Jesus was steeped in the Wisdom Literature at his disposal, especially the book of Proverbs. A close study of his sayings shows how he used it as the basis for much of his teaching. We choose to focus attention on this part of the total legacy available to Jesus for three reasons. First, this portion of scripture is seldom studied seriously and it has much that is helpful for our instruction. Second, Wisdom Literature reveals how the rabbis of later centuries modified the law to make it more humane. Third, wisdom literature has resonance with the Episcopal tradition, as we make common-sense revisions to our ethics, the way Jesus did.

Our thesis is that the Episcopal Church is very much in the tradition of Jesus as we rethink our position on homosexuality, redefine our stance on the election of a gay bishop and consider the official blessing of same-gender unions. We rely in part on common sense reason that flows from a new understanding of homosexuality and on added insight into the injustice we have perpetuated. When we apply the "love your neighbor" norm taught by Jesus we find it necessary to modify traditional tenets of the Church. We do not apologize, because we believe that we follow the example of Jesus who taught us the necessity of revamping ancient laws. For Episcopalians reason is one of the three legs of our famous stool. It is the important bridge that connects tradition and scripture to the modern world. We will show that Jesus used that precise bridge as he read the same Hebrew Bible that we read and then formulated his ethic of love.

CHARACTERISTICS OF WISDOM LITERATURE

Prudence and rationality were characteristics of Hebrew Wisdom Literature. Its purpose was to make the law acceptable and useful in every day life. Wisdom writings interpret the law, not to force rigid adherence, but to understand the reasons for it and thereby make it easier to apply on a practical level that really matters. Moreover, by use of simple, pithy sayings people could readily remember and understand. To put prudence into the words of a Proverb, "One is commended for good sense, but a perverse mind is despised."[54]

A major component of the Law was the requirement of almsgiving as a way of providing for the poor, the weak, the foreigner, and the outcast. The task of religious teachers was to impress on each generation "why" generosity is necessary and blessed by God. "Happy are those who are kind to the poor."[55] "Those who oppress the poor insult their Maker, but those who are kind to the needy honor him."[56] "Whoever is kind to the poor lends to the Lord, and will be repaid in full."[57]

Jesus adapted many of the characteristics of Wisdom Literature to his own teaching style.

(1) Wisdom Literature took a commonly understood law such as an eye for an eye, and then stated it in such a way as to give it new meaning. "Hate stirs up strife, but love covers all offenses."[58] "Those with good sense are slow to anger, and it is their glory to overlook an offense."[59] Jesus built his teaching on Wisdom Literature when he said, "Do not resist an evil doer. But if anyone strikes you on the right cheek, turn the other also."[60]

(2) Wisdom Literature often emphasized a point by exaggeration. "Better a dinner of vegetables where love is than a fatted ox and hate with it."[61] Jesus also used exaggerated contrast, "First remove the log out of your own eye and then you will see clearly to take the speck out of your neighbor's eye."[62]

(3) The Proverb appealed to good sense, as any moral virtue must seem reasonable. "Fools show their anger at once, but the prudent ignore an insult."[63] Jesus appealed to common sense when

he said that the wise man builds his house on a
rock foundation rather than on the sand.[64]

(4)   The mark of a wisdom saying is that it does not
need to be argued or explained. The precept
stands on its own as being self-evident. Once
a person sees the point, she or he is bound to
agree. Therefore, a wisdom saying did not need
to quote its legal basis; it was evident in its own
right. Similarly, Jesus did not invoke divine
authority in most of his teachings, as did most
of the prophets. What he taught was not true
because the law required it; it was inherently
true. He spoke with authority and what he said
had a ring of authenticity.

While Jesus used the style of Wisdom Literature
and based many of his teachings on Proverbs, he also
challenged wisdom teachings that he felt were dated. He
responded in a new way when a saying was no longer
appropriate as an expression of prudent love. We turn to
the Sermon on the Mount for illustrations. Our purpose
is to get a sense of how Jesus approached the issues of his
day, relying on Hebrew scripture, taking into account
and building on much of the tradition, but proclaiming
new solutions when the old wineskins were worn out and
needed replacement.

SERMON ON THE MOUNT: NEW PRUDENCE

The Sermon on the Mount is a study in blessing.
"Blessed" is a universal form in Wisdom Literature.[65]
There are nine beatitudes in the Sermon on the Mount.
In Luke, the first four blessings are directed to the poor,
the outcasts, those in grief, and those who are being

persecuted. These were persons who did not choose their lot, and could not avoid the circumstances of their lives. Note that Jesus changed the focus of wisdom literature. In Proverbs the sayings are addressed to the middle class, to those who have more direct control over their lives, while in the Sermon on the Mount Jesus addressed the poor who appeared to be without power.

In this Sermon, the poor person has no money to pay for a bond so that he can be released from prison until his trial. In that culture, a poor person often left his coat as his bond, his surety. Jesus told the poor people to overflow in generosity. If the person is required to leave his coat, leave his shirt also.

The Roman occupiers often required subject people to serve as means of transport for goods. A middle-class person when pressed into service might send his servant and his donkey. But a poor man, who owned no donkey, had to carry the burden on his back. Jesus told the poor man to carry that load for two miles if he were required to carry it one mile. This and the many other teachings in the beatitudes build on the tradition of Wisdom Literature, but go far beyond it. The "new prudence" taught by Jesus was that the only way powerless people can gain power is to find it within themselves. Jesus said these poor, oppressed people exerted great moral power by being better persons than their oppressors! Even in poverty or servitude they could express *agape* love, which in the end is a power greater than that of Caesar.

Time and again Jesus broke with the law of the Old Testament. "You have heard it said…but I say…." This form of teaching was a device that took the old law with all of its ancient clarity, held it up for consideration, and then gave it a new meaning. As an example, let us take his teaching on sexuality. Jesus reminded his hearers that the Law forbids adultery. His retort to a questioner was, "If a man looks with a lustful eye, he has already committed adultery."[66]

Jesus chose the sharp, sensational saying, using it with exaggeration, as he almost always did, to make his point. He drove his point home by calling a lustful look the equivalent of adultery. Matthew followed that saying with Jesus' words that it is better to jab out your eye or cut off your hand than choose a path that leads one to Gahanna.[67] This was a literary device, an exaggeration, to make a point. Certainly no law or community standard could be devised to accommodate this saying. The point was that our inner thoughts are important and help define who we are. There may be grave consequences to flirtations and sensual daydreaming. Do you want inner power, the power of God's Spirit? Then control your thoughts as you live out the gospel of real love, and you will have power from above even though your lot in life appears to make you powerless.

Now let us look at Jesus' words on divorce. "It was also said, "Whoever divorces his wife, let him give her a certificate of divorce. But I say unto you, whoever divorces his wife, except on the ground of unchastity, causes her to commit adultery; and whoever marries a divorced woman commits adultery."[68]

We need to sense the moral climate as the background for Jesus' words. Jesus quoted the seventh commandment, the prohibition against adultery.[69] The legal penalty was death for a woman caught in adultery. Society had determined that the social consequences of adultery and childbearing outside of marriage were so damaging that they could not be tolerated. But, again, both polygamy and divorce were legal for the male, and sex outside of marriage was legal, except with another man's wife or with a virgin. But, unchastity in the wife was grounds for divorce or even death. However, in this moral climate that accommodated promiscuity and divorce, the ideal of monogamous marriage for a lifetime was still strong in Hebrew society. The Proverb put it clearly, "He who commits adultery has no sense and he that does it destroys himself."[70]

Proverbs spoke of the value of a good and prudent wife[71] but also noted "a wife's quarreling is a continual dripping of rain."[72] Proverbs were all spoken from a male perspective. Note further, that all of the laws were designed to provide the widest freedom and latitude for the man and place the most restrictions on the woman. The response of Jesus was meant to protect the woman. The law of love brought equality into marriage.

Jesus saw marriage from a woman's perspective because the marriage codes were unjust toward her. He saw the situation in the way that love required. He who divorces his wife makes her the victim of adultery. Divorced women usually had no means of financial support, unless they could find another husband. It was commonplace for such women to become prostitutes as their only means of livelihood. Once again, Jesus shifted the focus from the strong to the weak. He said, in effect, that any system that permits the strong to exercise control over the weak is wrong. But it is also a plea for the strong to change their attitude toward the weak, so that justice prevails and respect is established.

In summary, Jesus spoke primarily but not exclusively to the powerless with a single message: You have the power to control your inner attitudes. Indeed, with a rigid social order, and with Roman rule firmly in place, the only control you possess is inner attitude. But, in the end you possess a power greater than that of Rome, if you accept the invitation to use it as part of the new kingdom. You have the power to love, albeit, this power is a gift from God. And the strong among you have the power to accept and assist the weak in a community of solidarity.

JESUS AND CONTEMPORARY SECULAR ETHICS

In a secondary sense Jesus was probably influenced by contemporary Roman culture and the Greek philosophers, who provided Rome with much of its wisdom. There was an affinity between the Wisdom Literature and Greek philosophy. Roman youth from prominent families were sent to academies to study philosophy, including Jewish wisdom literature. In Greek philosophy of the time, the "good action" was the "sensible" action.

In all probability Jesus lived in Nazareth during "the silent years" from the time he was twelve until his public ministry began. Some of us recall visiting the ancient inn that was standing in the time of Jesus. Nazareth was directly on the trade route between Cairo and Damascus. The inn was not a modern hotel. Rather, it was a rectangular enclosed wall with a gate in one end. At the other end was a flat roof, which provided cover over a third of the space. The enclosure below was reserved for camels, their cargo, and at times, sheep or goats. The caravan people slept on the roof, so they could keep a half-closed eye on their cargo and animals.

But the more fascinating insight is that Jesus grew to manhood living along an international trade route. The people he met and the ideas he encountered may have disposed him toward looking beyond Israel to the larger world.

Socrates, the master teacher, gave his life by drinking the bitter poison rather than recant his beliefs. He engaged the young men of Athens by asking questions rather than giving pat answers. The theme of his teaching was to know oneself. We note that Jesus, the master teacher, constantly asked questions and explored self-understanding. Like Socrates, Jesus went to his death willingly.

Plato proposed two kinds of *eros* love. Both were love of self, but one was "vulgar" and the other was "heavenly." He taught that over time vulgar *eros* leads to a debasement of personhood and hence of society. In vulgar *eros*, persons use others for their own satisfaction, with the strong, as a matter of course, taking advantage of the weak. Heavenly *eros*, on the other hand, while self-love also, takes a disinterested perspective and asks what is the greatest good for the greatest number as a society. Benefits may not be as apparent in the short term, but those who seek to live by heavenly *eros* are the truly prudent. Consideration for the entire social fabric is strengthened, and hence all are benefited in the long term.

In some ways Jesus and Zeno, founder of Stoicism, taught similar approaches to life. Zeno believed that self-control was the highest virtue. He taught indifference to the larger world in the sense that nothing should matter too much. The only path to happiness for him was to accept what exists and desire nothing more. In that way no person outside of oneself can control his or her happiness. The person who desires nothing needs nothing. He or she cannot be bought or sold. One can have wants but not desires. One can become rich so long as riches are not too important. The philosophy had wide appeal in a frightening and unstable world.

There was an enormous difference, however, between the teachings of Jesus and any of the Greek philosophers. Socrates taught, "Know your self." Plato taught, "Love your self." Zeno taught, "Control your self." Jesus taught, "Give your self." Jesus may have incorporated insights from the Greek philosophers, but he went beyond them. He issued the invitation to live under the reign of God and give oneself in love to the needs of others, as God, through his grace, gives himself for us.

JESUS AND LOVE FOR ENEMIES
Jesus presented the injunction to love your enemies and pray for persecutors.[73] He was not the first to point out that love was the profound moral principle that underlay the legislation in the Pentateuch, the first five books of our Old Testament. The prophets expressed the principle as they preached justice for the poor and others who were oppressed. A God who loves all people requires justice to keep some of his sons and daughters from taking advantage of others.

But Israel also had enemies. How were they to be

treated? The Jewish laws relating to war permitted, even required, Israel to be ruthless toward captured enemies. "…you must utterly destroy them. Make no covenant with them and show them no mercy."[74] It was altogether appropriate to hate your oppressor.[75] On the other hand, a person from an enemy land who was not involved in war was to be shown compassion, if that person were in need. "When you come upon your enemy's ox or donkey going astray, you shall bring it back."[76] And, again in Proverbs, "Restore a strong ox, even if it belongs to your enemy."[77]

Jesus carried love to a new level. He declared that vengeance belongs to God, not to humans. He taught that we exercise the highest freedom and therefore the greatest power by returning good for evil. As always, Jesus took the extreme example. In Luke we hear Jesus say, "Love your enemies, do good to those who hate you, and bless those who curse you. Pray for those who abuse you."[78] Again, these are maxims, pithy sayings, like proverbs. They appeal to an inner moral sense.

Jesus had enemies who challenged his teachings and put them to the ultimate test. They plotted against him in an effort to discredit him. Judas, a disciple, consorted against him and betrayed him. The crowds shouted, "Crucify him." Roman soldiers nailed him to a wooden cross to die, a painful, lingering death. All that Jesus said about enemies who mistreated him was his prayer from the cross, "Father forgive them, they know not what they do."[79]

How could this way of "agape" (impartial, self-giving) love make sense? The answer was clear for Jesus. It is the nature of God. God makes his sun to shine on the just and the unjust.[80] Note how Jesus departed from the wisdom literature, which claimed that the righteous are more blessed than the wicked. Jesus explained that the nature of God is generous and impartial. The sheer goodness of God is revealed to us in his mercy toward us all. "...for he is kind to the ungrateful and the wicked."[81]

Note again that Jesus reserved his severest criticism, even wrath, for the Scribes and Pharisees. Time and again he said, "Woe to you...you hypocrites." Always the reason was the same. In their harsh judgment of others, they were creating barriers that kept people from God. Instead of rejoicing at signs of the coming of the kingdom, by their prejudice, by their pretense at goodness, and often by their acts of injustice they set themselves up as the judges of others. "They devour widows' houses and for the sake of appearance say long prayers."[82]

Matthew wrote to a Jewish audience and he could take for granted their knowledge of the Law. Luke wrote to a Gentile world, which did not understand the obligation to meet the needs of the poor and oppressed. The Gentile world to which he wrote had little social conscience. Luke, therefore, used examples to show how to "do" good. In Luke this meant deliberately breaking with social conventions to show solidarity and generosity to all in need and to all social outcasts. Jesus appealed to the potential that lies in the human spirit. He challenged his followers to be accepting, fair, and forgiving. Jesus ended the Sermon on the Mount with a reflection on Leviticus, "You shall be holy, for I, the Lord your God, am holy."[83] Matthew concludes the sermon with the words of Jesus, "Therefore, you shall be perfect, as your heavenly father is perfect [holy]."[84]

Jesus, once again, took the extreme to make his point. God is not called "perfect" in any Hebrew writing. And it was blasphemy to consider any person as perfect. In the Greek Septuagint "blameless" is translated as perfect. Jesus is saying that the best moral conduct is that which imitates the nature of God. The nature of God is accepting, inclusive and loving. It is the special mark of God's nature to care for those who are mistreated by society because of prejudice or social class.

Jesus revealed the nature of God by appealing to such persons and speaking words of comfort and hope to them. The entire Sermon on the Mount sums up Jesus' understanding of the Law and the Gospel. Here is expressed the deepest meaning of love in action. The message reveals the power that God offers to the weak over the strong and reveals his strategy for changing the world into the kingdom of God. His words give hope and joy to the oppressed and despised.

THE GOOD SAMARITAN: DOING LOVE

We shall not do an analysis of the parables of Jesus. However, we shall look briefly at the story of the Good Samaritan, as it is in answer to the lawyer who had properly discerned the underlying ethic of Jewish law by saying it encompassed love for God and for neighbor. But then the attorney went further and asked, "Who is my neighbor?"[85] That is an important question because our human tendency is to limit neighbors to persons like us.

After two religious officials passed by the wounded man at the side of the road, a Samaritan who was journeying there, stopped, bound up the unfortunate man's wounds, and took him to an inn. He paid for his care and urged the staff to do what was needed for the wounded man, promising to pay on his return journey. Then Jesus asked the key question, "Which one of the three was neighbor to the man who fell among thieves?" When the attorney gave the obvious answer, "the one who showed mercy," Jesus said, "Go, and do likewise."[86]

Jesus took his stories from contemporary life, much like we are taking ours from the morning news. Each parable was designed to make a point. It was the despised foreigner who happened to be living by the law of love, more than the respected Jewish leaders.

Again, we note how Jesus dealt with Jewish law found in the Pentateuch. He respected this law but he also realized that it was dated and was being applied wrongly. Religious leaders were searching for simple clearly defined "do's and don'ts" to govern their moral lives much like so many people in America do today. They were asking for a literal inerrant reading of Hebrew scripture. Jesus rejected that approach, asked his followers to live by the law of love and do whatever the circumstance required. He dispensed with the prevailing customs and assumptions about right and wrong and cut to the core of what a loving God requires. We can do the same and thereby recover our basic Christian fundamental, our love for each other. How do we proceed?

GETTING TO KNOW THE MIND OF JESUS

Our challenge is to take the approach used by Jesus and apply it to specific issues with which we must deal. We are not repealing the teaching of Jesus; we are seeking to be faithful witnesses. How do we get from the first century to the twenty-first? How can we discern what Jesus would say or do if he were here grappling with our issues? Specifically, "What is the mind of Christ in the debate over acceptance of gays and lesbians?"

First we must really get to know Jesus the man, the teacher, the spiritual guide. We cannot be content to preach a formula, a doctrine of atonement or resurrection apart from the life and teachings of Jesus. These most important doctrines make sense only in the light of his ethic.

The process of new birth for us is to begin by standing back and analyzing his life and teaching, even keeping a critical distance in order to be objective. But at some point we must engage Jesus and enter into dialogue with him. Then we are led to "repent and believe the gospel" and "enter into the joy of our Lord."

At that point our identity shifts. We no longer ask, "Who am I?" but rather, "To whom do I belong?" Jesus said that we belong to God and to the whole human family. But for us as Christians, this belonging is realized through Jesus and we come to call him "our Lord." We then make it our mission to live into the stories and teachings of Jesus and follow the way he lived.

We are not content with superficial answers or rote teachings. First we try to more fully understand the context of Jesus' teaching, including the culture of his time and the relevant lessons from the Hebrew Bible. On the contemporary side, we seek new scientific knowledge as we analyze the particular circumstances that require justice and the application of agape love. Working in humility, in community, and under the guidance of the Holy Spirit, we discern how Jesus would respond now.

This requires disciplined imagination. It is not

fantasy, as some critics contend, but the opposite. Fantasy fabricates to avoid reality; imagination engages reality. We hear Jesus' command, "Go and do likewise."

SUMMARY AND REFLECTION

Who is the homosexual person in this Good Samaritan parable? Is he the Samaritan? Society projects the same kind of loathing and prejudice toward gay and lesbian persons as Israel projected on Samaritans. Do we stand in solidarity with gay and lesbian outcasts as Jesus did which such people? Are we ready to reinterpret Old Testament law in the same way Jesus did? Are we angry with those who keep gay and lesbian persons from God and full participation in the Church of Jesus Christ?

Others say the homosexual person is the victim left at the side of the road half dead. According to the FBI there were 9,500 victims of violent hate crimes in 2004. The most crimes were against African Americans with 3,475 listed. Homosexual persons ranked second with 1,428 documented cases of violent crime perpetrated against them. Either way, Jesus commended the Samaritan, a despised minority person who expressed compassion for the victim.

It is within this context of Jesus' teachings that we decide about accepting gay and lesbian persons into our churches, our hierarchy of leadership, and into every facet of civil society. Here are persons made in the image of God, as are those of us born as heterosexuals. They are born with a predisposition for attraction to persons of the same gender, and they comprise between five and ten percent of the population. What word of grace and hope does the Church speak to them?

Has the Episcopal Church, by its action at General Convention, been in the tradition of Jesus? Have those who oppose acceptance of such persons been in the tradition of the Scribes and Pharisees? Do we need a specific word from Jesus on homosexuality to verify the nature of God's love? Do we need to recite a verse of the Law to prove that homosexual persons should be excluded from full acceptance?

The Sermon on the Mount can surely be read as directed to gay and lesbian persons who have refused to remain in second class status as victims and have risen to overcome rejection and injustice. Those who refuse to hate or strike back with revenge enter the church as loving disciples and true witnesses to the message of Jesus. They are helping overcome one of the last major categories of discrimination in church and society. Blessed are they.

Look at a final injunction in the Sermon on the Mount: "Judge not and you shall not be judged." It is the spirit with which we judge that makes the difference. Jesus said another time to beware of wolves in sheep's clothing. He was not saying that we should ignore moral discernment. What he seems to be saying is that we should avoid adopting rigid, unloving attitudes through our judgments. Judge in love. Notice carefully the words used by Jesus. "He who is merciful to others, the heavenly father will be merciful to him." [87]

Friends in the faith, this is serious business.

All Wisdom Literature assumes that we can learn from the past, and let the past provide guidance for the present. Jesus incorporated this role of tradition as he formulated his own ethic of love. But he went beyond the traditions of Wisdom Literature and beyond the Law of the Hebrews. He used reason as found in the law of love to open new possibilities. He taught us to pray, "Your kingdom come on earth, as it is in heaven." We do not need to accept entrenched injustice. We do not need to continue living with things as they are. God is at work. As each injustice is battered down, we are invited to see it as a "sign" of the coming of the Kingdom. We are challenged to respond as if the God of love is King. Let those of us who are "straight" recognize the kingdom and enter, but as gracious citizens, let us step back and let gay and lesbian persons enter first.

Chapter 7
RIGHT AND GOOD IN CHRISTIAN ETHICS

"He who can put his finger upon that which
divides good from evil is he who can touch the
very hem of the garment of God."
—Kahil Gibran[88]

We have affirmed from the witness of Jesus' own
words that his ethic was based on a single principle of
love for God and neighbor. By his response to a lawyer's
question Jesus erased all of the prescriptive laws of
Israel. He taught a new way to live, a joyous adventure
into the kingdom of God. While this bold and sweeping
perspective is absolute, it is, nonetheless, incomplete.
An ethic requires principles and guideposts if not legal
prescriptions. What, then, is the moral compass for living
as a Christian in a complex world?

We begin with the observation that all people are
moral.

This is a moral world in the sense that all people in
all cultures have values. Every society has regularized
ways of getting things done. All have laws that govern the
actions of people, including ways to punish wrongdoers.
People everywhere believe that some acts are good and
others are bad. We express our values in the decisions
we make, even when these decisions are inconsistent. In
one role we use one set of values and in another we use
differing, even opposing values. A business man may, for
example, trick or cheat his competitor, yet in his own
home be both honest and kind.

The Mafia as, depicted in the popular television series, has as rigid an ethic as can be found. While its code permits members to take what they want through extortion from people they choose to exploit, yet the Soprano "Godfather" is loyal to members of his "family" and sometimes doting over his own children.

All people have values and judge themselves by how well they live up to their ideals. But you respond correctly, the Mafia ethic is not what we mean by "the moral life" in the usual sense of the term. Ordinarily we call that person moral who lives by the highest standards of humaneness. That sensitive and consistently responsible person each of us knows has higher moral values than the Mafia member. Yet both have standards and each judges himself by how well he or she lives by them.

The only person who has no sense of right and wrong is one whom psychologists call a psychopath. He or she can hurt others with impunity or commit any crime and feel no remorse. But such a person is pronounced sick and, therefore, is not subject to the law as a responsible person. That is to say, she or he is not deemed to be moral. These persons are excused in courts of law from moral responsibility. Others with mental illness may know the difference between right and wrong but be driven by inner forces they cannot control. Each of us except the psychopath has a conscience, which puts us in touch with our sense of right and wrong. As human beings with dignity and intelligence we know we have an inherent responsibility to do right and avoid wrong. It is this understanding of "natural law" that informs our Declaration of Independence and Constitution.

THE CHRISTIAN VOICE OF CONSCIENCE

As Christians we raise natural law to a higher level and affirm that our conscience is the Holy Spirit speaking to us. Our conscience is an inherent intuitive awareness of the moral imperatives we come to know in scripture. Karl Barth once observed, "The conscience is the perfect interpreter of life." Yet we also know that our conscience is fallible. We may place higher value on the teachings of our culture than on the love ethic of Jesus, our ultimate authority. Psychologists also point out how our conscience is often the "thou shalt nots" of parents or culture ingrained in us by social conditioning. They make lucrative livings by helping clients work through their hang-ups about feeling guilty for violating unreasonable requirements of their parents or unreasonable expectations they impose on themselves. The freedom by which Christ has set us free is inhibited by such an overactive conscience.

Can we agree on a basic understanding of conscience? The conscience is a faculty which helps us move outside ourselves, view ourselves objectively, and make judgments about the quality of our actions. Our conscience is fallible and can lead us to inadequate moral conclusions, yet we respect it as the touchstone of morality and act on the basis of the moral awareness we have at any given time. We conclude that even those who are religious persons must constantly question their consciences and strive to refine the sense of moral judgment.

What guideposts are there to mark our path as we refine our conscience? Historically, there have been two questions in ethics: What is right? What is good? Ethical systems are built upon one or the other of these questions, or a combination of the two.

DOING WHAT IS RIGHT

Those who adhere to an ethic of doing what is right say there are certain immutable laws of God written into human nature, certain first principles, which we are called to obey. We posit as first principles the Ten Commandments which deal with one person's relationship to another. To take an example, we say that murder is wrong. It is never "right" to kill. Therefore, regardless of the consequence to ourselves or to others we will hold human life sacred, and never kill another person.

Immanuel Kant built a formidable system of ethics on the "moral ought" and the principle of right intentions. He taught that when one intends to do what is right and follows right principles, one has fulfilled his/her responsibility. Kant did not consider results to be of ethical concern, only right motives in obedience to principle. For Kant there was nothing absolutely good except a person's good will. The principle by which this good will is to be expressed is this: So act that your deed may become a universal law.

Murder is wrong, he taught, because if done universally and without severe penalty it would destroy society. Therefore, regardless of the consequences, one does not take the life of another. Again, one must always be truthful and never bear false witness. Integrity is a fundamental quality of life. All human relations break down if persons cannot depend on each other's truthfulness.

A problem we face in Kant's ethic and that of "absolutists" within our Christian faith comes when more than one moral imperative is present in a given situation and these absolutes are in competition with each other. If we follow one moral duty without question, we may have to deny another valid principle. Suppose that we are in Iraq and are housing a person sought by a militia of Osoma bin Laden. A terrorist comes to our house with other armed men and asks if the person he seeks is there. If we are honest, our response will cause the victim to be killed. Should we lie to protect the life of an innocent person? Kant's answer was "no" because it is never right to lie. Others disagree and say that since life itself is of greater value than telling the truth, on a given occasion it is better to deceive the terrorist.

The conscientious objector to war may base his or her position on the absolute prohibition of killing. Many Quakers say that Jesus taught the sanctity of life, the power to overcome evil by being killed rather than kill. No matter what might happen to a person when confronted by a killer, it is better to die than to take the life of another person. Under no circumstances should one person deliberately kill another.

In much the same way the Roman Catholic Church takes the position that abortion is killing and there is an absolute prohibition against taking a life. The principle of protecting life is absolute. No other consideration can be brought into the equation.

DOING WHAT IS GOOD
This brings us to the second question in ethics: "What is good?" When we ask that question we are

concerned with outcomes rather than motives. English philosophers Jeremy Bentham and John Stuart Mill, among others, reacted to Kant's emphasis on doing only what is right by developing an alternative ethic based on what is good. The ethic of "utilitarianism" recognizes the relativity of values and insists that we must compare one good with another. No particular good is ultimate. The good, however, is not just what is good for me, but what is the greatest good for the greatest number of people. When protecting the person sought by the terrorists one must also be concerned with consequences. Kant was right in saying we should always focus on principles and approach every moral decision with good will; he was wrong in saying that only good intentions are ultimately good. The consequences of our decisions are equally important.

How do we reconcile these two approaches to ethics? How do we honor both intentions and consequences, what is right and what is good? The late H. Richard Niebuhr, Professor of Christian Ethics at Yale University Divinity School, was most helpful at this critical juncture. He suggested that the two approaches can support rather than oppose each other. The solution for him was a "both-and" rather than an "either-or." In his book *The Responsible Self*, Dr. Niebuhr argued that an ethical person must be concerned for right principles and for good consequences.[89] Good results are as important as good will. An ethical Christian person is concerned both for the act and the agent, for character and conduct. Responsible persons know that their action includes the whole train of consequences that follow from it and that these results must be taken into account along with the act itself.

DOING WHAT IS PRUDENT

With this balance we meet any given issue by evaluating not only what is morally right but also what is the greatest good for the greatest number. But the insightful ethicist noted that these two questions are often in conflict. To follow one approach is to deny the other. Therefore, Dr. Niebuhr added a third question: "What is fitting or prudent?" We deal creatively with each new situation because each time the factors are different. We believe that it is wrong to kill and it is right to preserve and enhance life. This is a bedrock ethical principle to which we are committed. In a given situation, however, other values must also be considered. A responsible person may decide to go into military service, kill or be killed, despite his deep conviction that it is morally wrong to kill, because a ruthless leader like Hitler is threatening the destiny of our nation and our civilization.

We may advocate birth control despite the biblical injunction to multiply and replenish the earth. At this point in time the earth's population has grown so large that it threatens to overwhelm the ecosystem so that it can no longer support higher forms of life. We must consider the consequences of our actions. Again, we honor the life of an unborn child and yet in certain circumstances we decide for an abortion because we recognize that giving birth would endanger the life of the mother, or create an overwhelming burden on the family. We are not flippant in advocating abortion, but we are not absolute in opposing it in every circumstance.

143

Oliver Wendell Homes once remarked, "I have trouble with men of principle. What I like to see are men with principles." His caustic words point up the difference between those who claim the luxury of standing on a single principle, as against those in responsible positions who must be concerned for many values at the same time.

The responsible self compares and weighs one value against another. Traditionalists scorn such a process and consign it to the wastebasket of "relativism." They imply that the person has no stable anchor, no core values, no eternal principles, and no recognition of eternal verities. Such persons are accused of drifting like the tides without stars to guide them.

As Christian moralists we do not go through a long process of analysis every time a decision is made. Usually we act in the moment in the way that seems best. Persons of character act spontaneously and intuitively, based on a lifetime of sensitive moral reflection. The result of our action is many times ambiguous; we may never know for sure that we made the right decision. We ask for God's guidance, make our best choice, and usually never know what would have happened had we taken a different course. This approach is more difficult than following a single principle without wavering because it requires us to choose, to take responsibility in the situation that presents itself. In short, it requires us to be prudent.

THE RESPONSIBLE SELF

The responsible self is the responding self. We respond to the proper demands of family, community, church, nation and world. We respond freely in a way that is our own and is unique to the circumstances. This approach never ignores the "moral ought." First principles are taken into account as significant when a course of action is adopted. But then, as Christians, we seek to know the mind of Christ and do what agape love requires. From this perspective the Christian ethic is creative and emergent.

This ethic, then, is not simply a set of fixed "immutable laws", driven deep into the structures of society to be applied rigidly and legalistically. Historically, our morals were encased in an authoritarian, ecclesiastical system. Traditional values grew from an agricultural economy, which was relatively stagnant. Stable circumstances led people to think in terms of unchanging moral laws. The ethic was prescriptive; both means and ends became rigid.

The opposite extreme is found in those who act simply on the basis of their feelings or on what they desire in the moment. Some want to bend all laws of justice or fair play if it works to their own advantage, quite apart from any reference to what is right or to the good of the greatest number. This path of expediency is as dangerous as a rigid, uncompromising moral system.

The middle ground of prudence or practical wisdom is to nurture our ethical sensitivity as we ask in each situation what are the right principles and what are the good consequences to be served. Today the rate of change in science, in evolution toward a single world system, or in our control over reproductive functions is so rapid that circumstances often outdistance our thinking. We are challenged to bring our ethics up to date, while holding firm to our basic ethic of agape love.

We illustrate the changing circumstances that

require different actions by considering birth control and the size of families. In traditional societies, many births were necessary to assure parents that they would have some children who would live to care for them in old age. In rural societies, the more prosperous families were the ones with more "hands" available to work the land. Today in many parts of the world the only insurance policy owned by a husband and wife is their children. So, while it is a crushing burden to rear a large family, it is, nonetheless, viewed as good and birth control is seen as bad. Now the values have shifted because medical science has increased the percentage of babies reaching maturity, governments have initiated systems of social security, and urban living does not require large families. Now small families are good because children are an economic liability rather than an asset. In addition, many responsible people believe that the world's population may soon multiply faster than food can be produced. What is good for society or for individual families has shifted to an almost opposite position from the traditional one. Birth control may now be necessary for the survival of planet earth. We still value human life and respect the dignity of every person, but we serve the greater good by limiting the size of our families.

Pope Benedict XVI gave a homily at the time of his elevation to pope. In that sermon he framed the central issue facing the Church as relativism. His predecessor had seen the issue for his time as that of confronting Communism with the truth of Christianity. Pope Benedict said that now the stark concern of the Church, especially in Europe and America, is relativism.

Indeed, he had written and released many official pronouncements of the Church on eternal principles versus relativism.

One such pronouncement condemned the government of China for adopting a policy of one child per family. The policy has now been in effect for some thirty years. The state supports and provides for birth control measures, and when they fail, abortion. The position of the Chinese government is that China has well over a billion citizens and limited amounts of food and other resources. It is the most populous country in the world. Should they follow the teachings of the Roman Catholic Church, the number of births would lead to the doubling of the population within a relatively short period of time. The consequence for the nation, as for most individual citizens, would be disastrous. The Roman Catholic Church accuses the Chinese of being relativists and failing to respect the conjugal responsibilities of married couples and the rights of the unborn. It grieves us when we feel compelled by our convictions to side with a secular state over a holy church, but many of us believe that the action of China more represents "the responsible self" than that offered by the Church of Rome. We wish the Chinese government would apply this law with more sensitivity and humaneness at times, but we affirm the intent of that law.

Anthropologists distinguish two types of values. There are descriptive values, which the objective outsider uses to understand what a culture is like. This approach presumes detached impartiality. The "descriptive" approach helps the outsider to understand the historical development of the culture's moral system and compare it with other value systems. The early Hebrew culture, in which a people is called by God into a covenant relationship, is, nonetheless, a relatively primitive culture, which can be studied and appreciated without considering it to be a full-blown ideal culture.

Beyond descriptive study there is the "normative" search for values, which is concerned with what "ought to be." Normative value implies that we can place right and wrong, or what is most humane and helpful, in a reality beyond preference or opinion. The existence of these values helps us establish objective standards by which the conduct of persons and cultures can be measured.

Traditionalists are correct in demanding eternal values that create moral conviction. We respond that the love principle of Jesus provides the Christian with three essentials: (1) clear guidance which keeps one from moral bewilderment, (2) objectivity which helps one resist the distortion of self-interest, and (3) conviction sufficient to inspire supreme effort and sacrifice.

On the other hand, relativists have important contributions to make. We find our moral compass not in static prescriptions but in doing what love requires in the situation. This "situation ethic" requires a responsible person to weigh and balance, to use reason and judgment. A lax moral relativism is dangerous, but so too is an inflexible reading of ancient values. The truth is that much of what we consider to be "normative" is actually our partial and ethnocentric perspective, based on unconscious assumptions not grounded in divine love. So, we are left with the burden and joy of discerning. We love God "with all our minds" and take the awful human responsibility God has granted—the responsibility to be prudent.

THE ETHIC OF INCLUSION

This rather lengthy exposition of the right, the good, and the fitting in Christian ethics provides the ethical framework for wrestling with the issue of homosexuality. What are the normative values revealed in scripture? Central to our response is the Jesus answer: "You shall love your neighbor as yourself." Supporting that central verity are other values which flow from "agape" love. Justice is God's concern for the equal treatment of all persons, which flows from the impartiality of God's love. Respect for the dignity of every person is based on the nature of God in the way we believe our Maker respects us. These reflections lead us to support basic human rights. When we respond to the worldwide Anglican Communion by saying that homosexual persons are entitled to human rights, some accuse us of providing a secular answer. Our Christian declaration of human rights is not just a secular manifestation embedded in international law through the United Nations, although that is important. We believe human rights are embedded deeply in the love ethic of Jesus. While we hope this ethic will inform civic life, we are not echoing a secular value. The kingdom of justice based on love leads us to conclude that homosexuality is a justice issue and it must be faced and reconciled with the basic human needs of gay and lesbian persons.

The entire thrust of this book is to contend that the "right" principles of justice, respect, acceptance of those that society considers as outcasts, and *agape* love all place inclusion of homosexual persons on that side of the ethical divide. Of course, those who still believe that the Bible teaches homosexuality as inherently evil believe it is "right" to oppose homosexuality. This still leaves open for both positions the necessity of determining what is "good."

The opponents of inclusion can believe firmly that their position is correct but still conclude that for the good of supporting the mission and harmony of the Church, they will accept the decision of General Convention. They may say to Bishop Robinson that they opposed his elevation to the role of bishop, but for the good of the Church they are resolved to work together. Such a response is based on the belief that the greater good consists in the positive work that can be done through the Church for the redemption of the world. Prudence leads the critic to cooperate.

The proponent of inclusion, on the other hand, may believe that in certain circumstances it is better to go slow and let the attitudes of conflicted church members catch up with the new understanding, rather than push ahead immediately with further reform. This could take the form of a moratorium of several years on elevating additional homosexual priests to the position of bishop. It might take the form of intensive dialogue with other members of the Anglican Communion over a period of years, or it might postpone the stamp of approval of lesbian and gay marriages. A church publishing company that believes strongly in the rightness of inclusion might still conclude that it represents all factions of the church and hence decide that the prudent position is to reject this manuscript at this time.

In any great social movement for justice there is always a role for the fearless prophets who proclaim "thus says the Lord." They take their clear stand for justice even when the conventional morals of the vast majority oppose their position. They go to the very frontier with their magnificent vision and drive down their moral flag.

Others in the role of priests or ministers come behind them with the mission of reconciling the majority one tiny step at a time to the new demand for righteousness. In the uncertainty that follows, some will be more courageous than others. Prudence for some will dictate that the advance must occur more quickly. They will speak and work actively to bring the kingdom of heaven to earth, even if a higher level of conflict is the price they must pay. Of course the natural human tendency is to want peace at any price, so the temptation to procrastinate is always present.

The battle is pronounced won at some point in every movement for social change. The position is confirmed by the majority in formal votes and pronouncements, and finally the Church moves on to deal with other moral challenges. We will not speculate now over what that next moral blind spot is with which we shall be confronted but we can be sure that God has more truth to spring forth from Holy Scripture and from the work of the Holy Spirit in our midst.

SUMMARY AND NEXT STEPS

To summarize, many of us believe that on the issue of inclusion for gays and lesbians, the lengthy debate has left the Church weary. Forty years of discussion, committees, study guides, and soul-searching at

General Conventions finally led to a decision to enter the promised land of inclusion. The Church by large majorities of bishops, priests, and laypersons has made its decision for inclusion. The need now is to consolidate this moral move forward and celebrate the fact that all are welcome in the Episcopal Church in the United States and in sister diocese extending through Central America to Venezuela. Nonetheless, those who believe that prudence requires a "go slow" approach for the sake of the greater good are to be respected and heard at the next General Convention. Again, the Church assembled will want to wait prayerfully for the guidance of the Holy Spirit.

This grand perspective helps us focus on what God requires and what by word and deed Jesus said love demands. Following Jesus is never easy, nor was it meant to be. Granted, the concept is new for many of us and old verities are challenged. Granted that we are asked to go beyond what we thought was sacred and find a new and larger meaning. But let us remember that is exactly the kind of thinking that Jesus did as he challenged old formulations of the law and reinterpreted what God requires.

A conclusion emerges from this cursory inquiry. We are all alike, created by God as members of the race called human. At the same time, we human beings in myriad cultural settings, religious traditions and varied educational levels respond to life in an almost infinite combination of patterns.

Each society has its own system of justice based on its cumulative wisdom and experience. But there is a sense of fairness written into the structure of life. All people require order and look to some kind of authority.

In times of confusion people often prefer an authoritarian government or an inerrant scripture to the responsible demand of being co-creators with God. In times of transition we find it hard to adjust our values to deal with emerging situations.

Every person desires the right to express his or her own personhood, even in oppressive cultures. Finally every culture has its vision of a better future. Some are more hopeful that others about the prospect of realizing their dreams. But everywhere there is a chasm between the real and the ideal worlds. Everywhere people who are true to the best in their religions are working to bridge that chasm.

There is a cluster of first principles, eternal verities, found embedded in God's Word. We believe that it is possible to build our Christian ethic on the fundamental truths of the gospel, while we also accept the truths of the great enlightenment and adjust our practices to take into account new insights. We build on right principles while insisting on good results. This approach saves us from recoiling in fear and being unduly defensive. Equally, it saves us from glib acceptance of the latest fad in values. One danger is rigidity; the other is shallowness. We accept the challenge to walk the middle way fed from the roots of our faith, enlightened by our noble traditions, and guided by the moral light of reason.

Chapter 8
THE WAYS OF GOD: A THEOLOGICAL PERSPECTIVE

Come Holy Spirit—from heaven
Shine forth with your glorious light
Come from the four winds, O Spirit
Come breath of God, and strengthen
Your people, Come Holy Spirit

To do theology is to discover and reflect on the ways of God. We gain theological insight by examining the way God worked among his people in the Old Testament. We enlarge our understanding as we find the new thing God did in the coming of Jesus as example, teacher, and savior. Our enlightenment expands further as we discover God at work in the early Church through the coming of the Holy Spirit. The question that engages us is whether God, in addition to setting down immutable laws of nature, gave us sacred prescriptions to be obeyed by his people for all time, or whether God is still leading and our understanding is emerging now and always. This chapter discerns anew the nature of the God we love and serve.

We believe the Episcopal Church in the United States is being guided by the Holy Spirit in an emerging revelation of the nature of homosexuality. But this conclusion should not surprise us if we establish that God is always creating something new. We are not interested in justifying a glib, changing popular culture at the expense of Christian morality. On the contrary, we seek to understand the ways of God in the Bible, in human history and in our day.

GOD DOES NEW THINGS

The Bible reveals a creative God. The book of Genesis begins with the all-important words, "In the beginning God...." The next word adds to the drama, "In the beginning God created...." Some insist that God had a momentary creative impulse and finished his creation in seven days. Others of us understand the single week of creation as a metaphor for God's ongoing and eternal creative impulse. Either way, our God is a creator. God created the heavens and the earth, the sky, earth and sea, all plant life on earth, and the myriad living creatures as they exist on our planet. And then God created the species we call human. But God was not finished when God made man.

In the Genesis account man was a solitary creature. At that point God realized that man had no helpmate. So God decided to create woman as a companion. At the same time, God designed a strategy for the perpetual replenishment of the human race in the sexual act of procreation. Then God issued the command, or invitation, to multiply and cover the earth. At that point humans became co-creators with God. We then entered an everlasting partnership between God and the human race. All that has transpired in the history of humankind is an account of that partnership between the creative action of God and people made in God's image, who also have the power to create.

The Bible is sacred, in part, because it contains the

story of God leading a people. Israel believed that God was involved in their lives. God inspired the laws they made and God changed his mind regarding some of those laws and then revised them. When certain laws no longer seemed appropriate, God gave a new prescription to better serve the needs of the people. This creative, all loving and all caring God leading his people is the real drama of the Old Testament.

The stories repeated by Jewish people from antiquity until today include the story of Moses and the way God used him to lead the people from Egypt, through the long wilderness journey, and eventually into the land of Canaan. God saw that the Israelites labored under the burden of slavery. God heard their cry as they groaned under the whip of the taskmaster. Then God remembered a covenant made years before with Abraham, Isaac and Jacob. So God went into action. God sought out Moses, now hiding in the land of Midian after he had killed a soldier who had beaten his tribal brothers. God caught up with Moses who was in a wilderness area tending the sheep of his father-in-law Jethro. Suddenly an angel of the Lord appeared to Moses in a fire, but the bush was not consumed. Then God told Moses to take off his shoes because he was standing on holy ground. Moses hid his face because he was afraid to look at God. God then stated why he had come. He wanted Moses to go back to Egypt and confront the Pharaoh, asking him to liberate the children of Israel. Moses objected. "Who am I that I should go?" But then God gave the assurance that lead him to accept: "I will be with you...."[90]

We pick up the saga in the wilderness where God is out front, leading Israel. The symbol is powerful and serves as a metaphor for all times. God led as a pillar of fire by night and a cloud by day. The God revealed to Moses was not a theological construct or a set of precepts, but the "living" God who was creating, directing, and eventually in a covenant relationship with these same Israelites.

Tobias Holler has done the Episcopal Church a great service by providing his insightful notes attached to *Let the Reader Understand: Principles of Scriptural Interpretation*.[91] He shows how on many occasions God guided, changed his mind, and decided issues based on the growing and evolving needs of the Israelites.

For example, many of us are surprised to realize that God began leading the human race by commanding that we be vegetarians. Adam and Eve ate fruit from the trees that grew in the Garden of Eden.[92] God confirmed the first great diet plan by saying, "You shall eat the plants of the field."[93] Then God relented. He changed his mind and permitted people to eat meat. The prohibition against meat was lifted after the flood, when Noah docked on dry ground. God said, "Every moving thing that lives shall be food for you, and just as I gave you the green plants, I give you everything."[94]

Lifting the prohibition against meat had a condition. Meat with blood on it could not be eaten. "Only you shall not eat flesh with its life, that is, its blood." God then issued a sacred warning lest the restriction be ignored. For those who failed to obey, "...I will surely require a reckoning."[95]

Let us follow the story of the "rare steak" to its conclusion. Eating meat with blood was one of the issues debated at the Council of Jerusalem in the early church when rules were being worked out as to what practices were necessary for Gentiles when they entered the Christian community. The Jewish Christians relented on the issue of circumcision, agreeing that the practice was not essential for Gentiles, but the conference concluded with a compromise. On the other issue of eating meat with blood, the decision was that this was too sacred an instruction for it to be discarded. The Gentile Christians agreed to continue the ancient practice.[96]

To carry this story to its conclusion, the Church in the west, which is the strand in our own tradition, broke from the Church in the east around many aspects of theology and practice. In the west, the prohibition related to eating meat with blood was dropped. However, in the east this prohibition continued and is the official practice of that branch of the Church to this day.

The Church fathers argued that the prohibition applied to one era of history, but in effect, God changed his mind and decided it was no longer applicable at a later time. The divine mandate was declared to be temporary, not part of an eternal order. Augustine of Hippo argued that since the Christian community of his day was composed almost entirely of Gentiles, it no longer made sense to observe this ancient Jewish law. John Calvin made the same point in his *Institutes*.[97] He concluded that the edict drawn by the Jerusalem Council was for "charity" so as not to offend Jewish Christian brothers and sisters. It was a political act to preserve harmony, not the confirmation of a divine command that applied for all time. Anglicans went further and noted that the Jerusalem church had erred in requiring this prohibition.[98]

We have followed this rather lengthy account to demonstrate the way God has worked in history. God led his people to embrace customs and laws that served the people well at a given time. But in different circumstances and at a later point in history God revealed to the community of the faithful that a different understanding was appropriate.

Tobias Holler uncovered another example of God changing his mind. He directed us to the book of Numbers in which inheritance laws were made and adjusted. When women were excluded from the right to inheritance some brave females came to Moses and pleaded their case. Moses consulted with the Lord, agreed that their cause was just, and then revised the inheritance laws so they would be included.[99] But, over time, it turned out that inheritance through women was being passed along to other tribes because women of one tribe were marrying men in other tribes. When Israelite tribal leaders objected, Moses again consulted with the Lord and the decision was made that the women had to marry within their own tribe in order to receive an inheritance.

This last example is a portrait of tribal society which had to adjudicate disputes. Moses as the great lawgiver is called upon in spirit to confirm and support tribal decisions. They fervently sought the Lord's will as they revised the laws to accommodate changing circumstances. God did not have a single set of laws eternal in the heavens. Rather, God worked with and through the people and culture to design and modify laws that best served their needs and interests.

The prophets of the Old Testament had the task of discerning the purposes of God at a particular time and of speaking forth that word of God both as reprimand and as vision. Their unquestioned assumption was that God was active, involved and leading his covenant people.

GOD'S NEW CREATION IN JESUS

This brings us to the New Testament, which again reveals God at work as creator. Here we encounter the same God, but now God is doing a new thing. The ever acting, moving, fulfilling God reveals his divine nature in the person of Jesus of Nazareth.

Now the whole human family, in the tradition of Israel, has assurance of what God is really like. Christians believe that Jesus was so in tune with the will and purpose of God that his life and ministry are not only an insight into the highest and best in human nature but also a revelation into the nature of God. The fervent prayer of Jesus in the Garden of Gethsemane has for us the ring of authenticity when in great agony he said, "Not my will, but yours be done." At every point in Jesus' ministry we see revealed the will of the greatest man, but also the will of God. There is no occasion where we see a discrepancy between what Jesus said and did and what we perceive was the will of God. The kingdom was fully present in Jesus. Here was God in human form.

We reverse the logic which says Jesus is like God and say God is like Jesus. The words of Jesus are for us the voice of God. The anger of Jesus strikes us as the wrath of God. The tears of Jesus are for us the pity of God. The special concern and tender care of Jesus for the poor, the outcast, the downtrodden is revealed through Jesus as the compassion of God. The years of patient instruction Jesus gave his disciples was intended for us also, because

God has ongoing work for us as co-creators. This same creating God now needs mature and full-grown persons—laity and clergy—with great wisdom to carry forward the compassionate work of the One who makes old things new.

GLIMPSES OF THE HOLY SPIRIT AT WORK

Jesus had promised the presence of God's spirit to the disciples after his death and resurrection. The Holy Spirit would come to comfort, to strengthen, and yes, to guide the band of followers as the early church formed and developed. The early church broke all bounds as the power of the Holy Spirit descended on the gathering in Jerusalem.

The Holy Spirit is depicted by symbols of light, fire, wind and breath. The God we worship through Jesus Christ is not a static God. Rather than understand scripture as immutable moral laws, the ancients more often tried to get glimpses of God's presence and purpose in parables, song, poetry and drama.

Every page of scripture seems to indicate that God allows us to learn, grow and change. It is an open question among theologians as to whether God changes his mind, or whether humans grow in their understanding of God. Certainly the Hebrew community believed that God did change his mind. We say with assurance that God does not change his mind about his divine intention for humanity, which Jesus stated clearly and succinctly: human beings should love God and one another.

The biblical revelation of God's creative nature suggests that God expects us to be active in our day in discerning the signs of the times and in re-creating ourselves as a holy people. God's agenda abides. God desires that the human race live in justice, harmony and peace. We are "on track" when in the baptismal covenant we ask that each of us "...respect the dignity of every person." There is unfinished business on God's agenda.

We conclude that scripture reveals changing moral codes that best serve people of each age. The deepest insight for us is that God calls "us" to be open to the new divine challenge. We go first to the bedrock of our faith in Holy Scripture. We honor the traditions that we have inherited. But this is our new day and God is still creating, revealing and moving ahead.

One part of our faith does give assurance that we are set firmly on the great rock of our salvation. We are established, with the security symbolized by our great cathedrals. But in another sense, we are always a pilgrim people. We are like Moses in Moab. We go forward following the fire and the cloud to our new land, which God will eventually show us.

SEXUALITY AND SIN

We next turn our attention to the relationship between sexuality and sin, recognizing the close link that has existed between the two throughout Christian history. This is not surprising because sin is so readily revealed in sexual behavior. First, sex is often used for self-gratification, without consideration for the welfare or fulfillment of the other. Unfortunately, it is women who have suffered the most. This occurs within the bonds of holy matrimony, as it does in the purchase of sexual favors in prostitution or in random sexual encounters. Secondly, sex is often used as an instrument of power.

163

This control often becomes institutionalized in social and legal practices. Women have traditionally yielded to the will of men and have accepted subservient status and roles because it is the lot of women to bear children and because they nurture and support them.

However, the relationship between sex and sin in marriage goes much further in Roman Catholic theology, which the Church of England inherited. Augustine articulated an understanding of the nature of sex in the fourth century. He interpreted original sin as innate sexual desire, which he equated with lust. Sexual expression is sinful because it is giving in to lust. He recognized, nonetheless, the necessity for procreation and therefore for marriage. However, he admonished married couples to use restraint in sexual practice within marriage, remembering that even marital sex is tainted by sin. Married couples, he wrote, should strive to limit intercourse to what is necessary for procreation and they should look forward to a mutual secession of sexual activities at the earliest possible time.

At no point does Augustine concede that marriage for Christians is a choice equal in sanctity to that of celibacy, a life without sex. Hence clergy and others committed to religious orders had, he taught, a higher calling and were not subject to sin in the same way as the common laity.

There is a carryover of this perspective into early Anglican theology. One of the Articles of Religion of 1801 is entitled "Of Original or Birth-Sin." It says in effect that we are sinful by nature because we were conceived in sin. "The flesh lusteth always contrary to the Spirit; and therefore in every person born into this world, it deserveth God's wrath and damnation." The Article recognizes that those in Christ can be saved from this damnation, yet it ends, "concupiscence and lust hath of itself the nature of sin."[100]

It follows, of course, that if the primary purpose of marriage is to conceive and nurture children, and if sex within marriage is unholy outside of the purpose of conception, then same-gender marriage could have no meaning or purpose.

For another century and a half after the Articles of 1801, the Episcopal Church continued to promote a restrictive marriage ethic in which sexual expression was only for procreation. Pleasure was still perceived as dangerous and men held authority over women.

Marriage is still male dominated today in many parts of the Anglican world, in the Roman Church, and in much Evangelical theology. Husbands and wives are partners and spiritually equal, but the man remains in charge. Marriage can be harmonious only when the wife understands that her role is to be an obedient subordinate and the husband an authoritive patriarch. In the theology of many churches today, marriage remains a gendered structure in which there is an inequality of power, status and privileges.

The Episcopal Church in the United States has updated its theology of sex and marriage. As in every revision of theology and liturgical practice, the change did not come without contention. Yet most of us believe that our new stand more represents the mind and will of Christ than did the old orthodoxy and it led directly to Episcopal ordination of women into the clergy.

WOMEN AS CLERGY: GOD DOES A NEW THING

This leads to a discussion of women clergy. The elevation of Cardinal Joseph Ratzinger to Pope Benedict XVI raises again the theological rationale for their exclusion from the clergy in the Roman Catholic Church. A new official pronouncement titled, "On the Collaboration of Women and Men in the Church and in the World" was released recently under the guidance of Cardinal Ratzinger.

The pronouncement states that God loves men and women equally. There is no gender difference in essential dignity. Then why can't women be ordained to the priesthood? The Church responds that sex differences are an essential component of God's plan for humanity. Man and woman are both parents, but one is father and the other is mother. These differences are constructive as each has a different, albeit, complimentary role.

The Church continues by presenting a biblical and then a theological rationale for limiting the priesthood to men. First, Jesus was male and he handed down the keys of the kingdom to men in the line of succession. But as important, the Apostle Paul likened the relationship between Christ and the Church to the harmony between a bridegroom and his bride. "Christ loved the Church and gave himself for it." Just as the bridegroom loves the bride, so Christ loves the Church.

The argument continues that the priest stands in the role of the bridegroom. He, therefore, has the awesome task of loving the Church and giving his life for it. What is the role of the woman? It is personified in Mary, the mother of God. Her essential role was to say "yes." She willingly accepted her call to be the mother of God.

The new pronouncement concludes that since men and women have different but complementary roles, and since the Apostle Paul gave us the inspired portrait of Christ as the bridegroom and the Church as bride, and since Roman Catholic popes, bishops and priests stand in the role of Christ, women cannot be admitted to the priesthood.

With sincere respect for the ancient and holy Roman Catholic Church, as non-Catholics, we are compelled to question this line of reasoning. We do not believe it provides a convincing rationale for the continuing exclusion of women from the priesthood.

The Apostle Paul used an analogy when he likened the relationship between Christ and the Church to that of a bridegroom for his bride. Any one of us who has experienced the tenderness, the love, the longing between man and woman at the time of marriage, can then by analogy imagine better the ways in which Christ loved the Church. The analogy opens for us an awareness of how we might give ourselves to Christ. But note that this is an analogy. One does not prove that women should remain subordinate to men in God-given leadership roles by using a figure of speech. Paul could have used a different analogy to convey the same truth. For example, he could have spoken of friends like David and Jonathon, who loved each other and were willing, if necessary, to give their lives for each other. The message was not the figure of speech but the truth conveyed by their words.

The crucial insight Paul provided us with this analogy is that Christ cared passionately for the Church.

He loved the disciples who formed that initial circle of believers. He cared deeply for those he touched and taught and transformed. These persons became the original *ecclesia*, the called out, the assembly, the Church. We believe that the resurrected Christ, seated at the right hand of God the Father, continues to love and inspire people today in human communities of called out persons who comprise the Church. There is no necessary or essential requirement here that church leadership be restricted to men.

The more basic question for the Roman Catholic Church is whether women are inherently unsuited for priesthood. Since the Church would never say that women are unequal in the way God loves them, it must say that the physical and psychological makeup of woman is different because of her God-ordained role as mother. She bears the child and has the subsequent primary role of nurture. That argument gets to the issue of whether God created woman for purposes so different that she can never be eligible for holy orders.

We affirm women and men to be equal in inherent qualifications for priesthood. Indeed, we believe that the experience of motherhood may be a gift that enriches her contribution as a priest, complementing the contributions of the male priests. We have a brief history with this experiment of women clergy. Our biblical response is one given by Jesus to a messenger who came from John the Baptist to Jesus. John was languishing in a dark prison. He began to wonder why Jesus had not declared his messiahship more forcefully and initiated the end of the age. So John sent his messenger to inquire if Jesus was the one who was to come, or should they look for another.

Jesus said, "Come and see." The lame walk, the blind see. Come and observe the works that I do. Let my ministry speak for itself.

The Episcopal Church in the United States took a bold step forward when we ordained women. We broke with tradition. We angered many of our members who honestly believed that we were ignoring scripture. And we bewildered the Roman Catholic hierarchy. Nonetheless, we are ready to evaluate our judgment as to whether it was from God. We say to one and all, "Come and see." Come and see the inspired leadership offered by many female clergy. Come and see the changed lives inspired by women priests, the broken hearts that have been healed through their ministry. Come and meet the bishops, the theologians, the President of a leading theological seminary. If this work is of God there will be fruits of the Spirit. Come and see the fruits that have been produced.

The Church was ready to confront the issue of homosexuality because it had been able to reform its doctrines on marriage and the ordination of women. In dealing with these issues the church concluded that all persons are equal in the sight of God, and that agape love requires respect and mutuality in privileges and responsibilities. It is interesting to note the close correlation between the rejection of women and their long struggle for inclusion for the priesthood on the one hand, and the rejection of lesbian and gay persons and their drive for inclusion for marriage and full standing within the Church on the other hand.

SHOULD HOMOSEXUALS BE EXCLUDED AS "UNREPENTANT SINNERS"?

We turn next to another theological issue that needs clarification. Some opponents of homosexual clergy believe advocates are proposing to welcome unrepentant sinners for the sake of inclusion. When we say that God loves all people and welcomes all persons into the kingdom, does the "whosoever will" mean they are invited to bring their sinful practices as well? The Rt. Rev. Francis C. Gray, Assistant Bishop, Diocese of Virginia, wrote a brief but cogent paper entitled, "Jesus and the Ethic of Inclusion." He points to a false assumption, that it is permissible to overlook sin in our modern desire to be inclusive. "It is often stated that Jesus welcomed all persons without regard to their moral situations, and such persons assume their sinful behavior will be welcomed as well."

Bishop Gray rightfully points out that Jesus did not accept a continuing pattern of sinfulness. There is no biblical justification for the church to institutionalize sin. He points out that a central theme of the synoptic gospels is summed up in Jesus words, "The time has come. The Kingdom of God is near. Repent and believe the good news." For the individual the good news was based on the willingness to repent.[101] Again, Bishop Gray points out that Jesus was inclusive in interacting with the woman at the well. He challenged her to give up her sinful ways and live in the Spirit. Finally, he reminds us that Jesus was inclusive when he invited everyone, "Come unto me all you who are weary and burdened and I will give you rest." But, he continued, noting there is a condition, "My yoke is easy and my burden is light."[102]

Bishop Gray concludes his article by reasoning that homosexuality was considered to be a sinful practice in Hebrew history and in the time of Jesus. Since our Lord never spoke favorably of it, Jesus must have agreed with the historical attitudes and practices of Judaism in his day and pronounced it sinful.

The essential assumption, therefore, is that homosexual behavior is always and under all circumstances inherently evil. That is the critical question. Does a person created by God as homosexual have a sinful nature different from the nature of heterosexual persons?

All of us agree that a central teaching of scripture is, in the words of the Apostle Paul, "All have sinned and fall short of the glory of God."[103] The Book of Genesis helps us understand the human condition from a theological perspective. We are created in the image of God as good. But by willful choice, we place our interests ahead of God's will, and so become fallen. We push God aside because we want to be God. All people sin, but it is the will and purpose of God to restore fallen sinful humanity to a state of goodness. We live in the tension between what "is" and what "ought to be." But prior to our sin, we are good, loved and accepted by God.

Some believe homosexual persons are inherently more sinful that others because they have chosen a practice forbidden by God. Others accept the view that their "condition," is given and not chosen but still believe the expression of homosexuality is sinful. They conclude that the homosexual person sins only when she or he practices acts of homosexuality. Could it be possible that a third view is more accurate? God accepts gay and lesbian persons as they are because that is the condition in which they were created. The entire debate revolves around the question of whether homosexual acts are inherently evil for people who were created by God with those inherent predispositions.

It is worth repeating that there is no evidence that scripture ever considered the option of faithful, monogamous homosexual relationships as a way of life. Biblical examples were based on the assumption of men taking advantage of boys or of other exploitative relationships. There is no evidence that the ancient world understood the innate sexuality that we now believe to exist. Yet it would be inaccurate to say that the Bible supported homosexuality or condoned its practice. What we can say is that we serve a God who provides us with new insights.

NEW INSIGHT MAKES OLD TRUTH UNTENABLE

We do not apologize for changing our position when the old one is discerned to be unjust and when it is wreaking untold harm on homosexual persons. The change in position is consistent with all that we know about the nature of God as revealed in the biblical record.

We have changed our positions many times when new insights have made old truth untenable. We have used as an example our evolving understanding of God's purpose in marriage. We have shown that the ordination of women to the priesthood is a step forward under God's unfolding leadership of his people. And, finally, we have examined the issue of inclusiveness with the conclusion that the Church should never institutionalize sin, but with the belief that the condition of homosexuality is given by God and therefore is to be honored by all persons. We find it exciting to be followers of the God of light, fire, wind, and breath.

Chapter 9
CHRISTIAN WORDS FROM HOMOSEXUAL PERSONS

> "God loves you just as you are. God cares for you. You do not have to deny anything about yourself. All you need to do is respond to God…. If you are in despair over your condition, God still loves you and accepts you as you are. It is the Love which in Dante's words 'moves the sun and the other stars.'"
> —*Christian Words to a Homosexual* by W. Norman Pittinger

If we are to debate and decide the fate of a significant portion of our congregations or potential communicants we should, at the very least, provide them a hearing. Too often gay and lesbian persons are ignored, talked about, voted on, discriminated against, and in many cases made unwelcome in our churches without being heard or understood. In some places they are objectified, stereotyped and treated as villains, rather than as fellow priests, our sons and daughters, or the neighbor down the street.

In this chapter the writer tells stories of gay and lesbian persons and samples their literature. He also invited a number of them to review this chapter and contribute to it. The words that follow are presented as if spoken by members of that community. Here are bits and pieces; a variety of individual colored stones that form a mosaic, hopefully a fair account of the gay and lesbian perspective. In short, the purpose of this chapter is to speak to the Church and to the public at large on behalf of homosexual persons, especially those who carry the name "Christian."

DEMOGRAPHIC STUDIES

How many of us are there in the population? There are hundreds of studies and yet it is difficult to give an accurate number. Responsible researchers are reluctant to give a definitive answer because our community knows that a majority of us still have never "come out" and declared our sexual identity. It is a safe bet to say there are more of us than you think.

A good starting place is with the number of households with same-gender relationships as reported by the U.S. Census Bureau, Census 2000. The census did not ask the sexual orientation of individuals, so there is no measure of the number of singles who are openly gay or lesbian. By adding together the male and female same-gender households, the census gives us a total of about 1,200,000 same-gender persons living as householders. In comparison, the 1990 census data showed only 145,000 same-sex unmarried households, or a total of 290,000 individuals. The dramatic rise in the number of households over ten years we attribute to the increased desire for long-term commitment on the one hand, and the willingness to report more accurately on the other.

A recent study of gay and lesbian voting habits conducted by the polling organization Harris Interactive determined that 30 percent of gay and lesbian persons are living in a committed relationship in the same residence.

Using that figure as fairly reliable, Harris estimated the gay and lesbian population at five percent of the total population over age 18. With a total population of 209,122,094 in the 2000 census, the estimated gay and lesbian population is 10,456,405. From the polling data Harris concluded there are 3,136,921 gays and lesbians living together in committed relationships in the United States. Note that this is three times the number reported in the official census.

Other studies have placed the number as low as one percent of the population, while some national organizations of gays and lesbians who want to influence the votes of political leaders estimate the total as high as ten percent. Some of us migrate to population centers where we can find a large community and where we can ease into gay or lesbian life without being noticed. Official data available in the U.S. Census showed that Los Angeles has the highest percentage of open gays and lesbians, with 9.77% of the population. Next was New York with 8.37%; San Francisco with 7.9%; Washington, D.C. with 4.42%; and Chicago with 3.65 % of the total population of the city recognized and reported as gay or lesbian.

The National Health and Social Life Survey (NHSLS) is a landmark research project from which two books were published. *Sexual Practices in the United States* is one of these books.[104] It has a chapter which focuses on the definition of homosexuality and provides studies of the incidence in the population. The study points out that one reason it is difficult to get agreement on prevalence is because various studies use differing definitions. This survey asked questions that covered five definitions: (1) Have you ever had a same-sex partner? (2) Have you had at least as many same-sex partners as opposite sex partners since the age of 18? (3) Have you had an exclusive same-sex partner for the past year? (4) Have you had an exclusive same-sex partner for the past five years? (5) When you think about sex is your desire directed toward your own sex or the opposite sex?

The survey found that 4.9% of men answered question two to indicate homosexuality, while women were at 4.1%. On question three, men were at 2.7% and women at 1.3%. The largest incidence occurred when asked about sexual desire where 7.7% of men desired male sexuality and 7.5% of women fantasized about females.

OUR NEED FOR ACCEPTANCE

At the end of the day it does not really matter whether we are five percent or ten percent of the population. We are present in every village, in every factory and in every profession. The discrimination is still there regardless of the numbers. Our need to be heard and accepted will not go away, whichever census data is correct.

Who are we and what do we think? First, thank you for asking! That is unusual in our experience, and in itself gives us a certain sense of dignity and respect. It is dangerous to make general assumptions about us. The only thing we have in common is our sexual orientation. For some reason we are attracted to persons of the same sex, rather than toward the opposite gender. Otherwise, as Will Rogers once observed, "Human nature is pretty well distributed throughout the race."

One trait that is universal among us is our felt need to be respected. We want to be connected to you, and indeed, to the whole body of Christ. We would like to be free to be drawn into the very inner circles of fellowship with you and into communion with God. We believe this desire is neither homosexual nor heterosexual, but rather a human desire, since we are created for each other and for God.

We are degraded when we are excluded, treated differently, and made to feel like second-class persons. This rejection pains us very deeply, especially in church, and most particularly, when the ostracism comes not just from individuals, but from the very canon law of the Church.

BORN THIS WAY

We are often asked whether we have chosen this lifestyle or whether it chose us. The question is fundamental to this discussion and lies at the heart of our case for inclusion. Is homosexuality at its basis a life-style choice for which participants should be held morally accountable? Or is it biologically determined by factors not yet completely understood, but involving genetics or *in utero* hormonal conditions? Is it a social preference or a biological given? If we were asserting a sexual choice, most of us feel we should still have that right. But if our homosexuality is a condition we were born with and discovered rather than a choice we made, we then cannot understand your condemnation.

The origins of homosexuality should be irrelevant to the debate over our acceptance. Yet it is a fascinating quest for us to delve into studies of inherited genes or different brain formation. Some reputable doctors still believe that homosexual orientation for a boy is formed in early childhood when he is dominated by a possessive mother and rejected by a passive or angry father. Some of this parental syndrome does occur, but in the experience of most of us, rejection by our fathers comes after they realize we are gay. Sometimes when our dads reject us our moms give us added protection and attention to try to compensate. We then absorb an added burden of guilt because we have created a rift between our parents.

We testify with almost unanimous voice that most of us were born this way. Granted, a small percentage of practicing gays and lesbians do so as a result of life-style choice. Granted, further, that there is a continuum all the way from those of us who are exclusively and forever gay to those who are bi-sexual to those who experiment for a time with a different orientation. In most instances, however, when it appears that we are "choosing" a new life-style, it is because we have been emboldened by the example of others and find the strength to declare openly who we are. We regularly ask each other: "Why would any sane person choose homosexuality when there is so much prejudice and discrimination against us? In a society in which we are despised, discriminated against and vilified, why would we choose such a fate?"

The fact is I don't need an answer from the genetics lab. I am gay. I knew that I was gay long before I knew the word "gay" or that the world had other people like me. I didn't choose to be gay. Like so many others I have met, I struggled for years with the awful reality that I was "different."

WAYS CHURCHES RESPOND

We observe that the church responds to us in a variety of ways. Some in the Episcopal Church—more in most other denominations—believe that any expression of homosexuality is sinful, and they want to exclude us until we reform. We note with profound sadness that recently the United Methodist Church affirmed the right of any parish minister to exclude gays and lesbians from church membership.

A much larger group welcomes us in the same way they welcome persons with an alcohol or drug addiction. They believe that our lifestyle problem is analogous to such an addiction. They say that when one becomes addicted, it is hard to break free, but the only way to a Christian moral life is to throw off the chains of addiction. We hear that some parishes offer counseling, prayer groups, and Bible study with the admonition to have faith that God will help us overcome the addiction.

This segment of the Church invites us to leave behind our obsession with homosexuality. Some would say that we must repent and about-face. Others revert to silence, but the silence speaks loudly. We are unacceptable to God and to the congregation until our life-style has changed. We are asked to give up this aspect of our identity or be consigned to hell. The choice for us is clear—give up our sexual orientation or be unacceptable to God and the Church of Jesus Christ.

In other settings, we can accept our "condition," but we must forego any active sexual expression. Celibacy forever has been what the Church traditionally has asked us to accept. What this means is not just abstinence from sex but also from love and from having a family. Some who counsel us liken this to the suffering of Jesus on the cross. They invite us to participate in Jesus' suffering, as we sacrifice our lives for him. Such would-be friends may be sincere but they are also cruel. The suffering of Jesus was for a noble purpose. He was rejecting enslavement by Rome and declaring the freedom of the human spirit to be loyal to God alone. He was reaching out in a great display of love to forgive his enemies. We do not see such noble purpose in our suffering.

These are not ways out of our distress, because they don't work. The prayer and the counseling do not cure our condition but only drive us into deeper despair. Further, we see parts of the church as blind and lacking a moral compass of their own when they say that promiscuity and prostitution have a moral value equivalent to living in a loving, committed same-sex relationship. Both are branded as living in sin. How can we navigate through such treacherous waters? We are compelled to conclude that in the eyes of these churches homosexual persons are not fully human.

I am part of a religious community where the infertile are counseled on how they might have children. The sick are held up before God in daily or weekly prayer. The wayward who return are welcomed like the Prodigal Son. But I find that in many places homosexual persons are not mentioned and indeed, are unmentionable. I listen to the silence. What doctrine is being articulated as I am ignored? If I were to raise my hand and say, "Excuse me, but I am here too," what word of hope do you have for me?

Other people in our Church claim that homosexuality is not so much a moral choice as a mental illness. Lesbian and gay persons need psychiatric help, they say. We respond that the American Psychiatric Association and the American Psychological Association removed homosexuality from its list of mental illnesses more than twenty years ago. They concluded that homosexuality is neither an illness nor a moral lapse. They now recommend that their members support same-gender marriage in the interest of maintaining and promoting mental health. Both organizations support same-gender civil marriages and take no position on church-related marriage.

By contrast, some psychiatrists still seek a "cure" for homosexuality, although the number is small who publicly make the case. The official term they use to describe themselves is "reparative therapists." The promise of rescue strikes a deep chord for many of us who feel trapped in our sexuality. These therapists say they are motivated by compassion for us. They assume that those of us who are gay can never find fulfillment with another man and that any attempt to do so becomes a pattern of self-destructive compulsion. They believe our whole pattern of behavior is inherently neurotic.

Follow-up after years of intensive counseling indicates that only one in four completes the therapy. Some of these do marry and maintain a stable marriage. More revert to homosexuality after their "white knuckle experience" of trying to be heterosexuals. Some testify that they have not lost their primary sexual attraction to men, but they have been able to accept the opposite sex enough to maintain a marriage. The American Psychological Association has concluded that for some it is possible to change behavior but not orientation.

Most professionals now feel that sexual orientation is as basic as left-handedness or blue eyes. However, the reparative movement, long thought to be discredited, is experiencing a resurgence. We draw a parallel with the teaching of creationism or with quack cures for cancer. Most of us believe the hope of a "cure" is a cruel hoax because our sexual orientation is part of our basic biological makeup.

We like to read about Troy Perry, the defrocked Pentecostal pastor who "came out" and told his congregation that he was gay. After exclusion from his denomination, in time, he founded the Metropolitan Community Church in California. At the founding service he gave testimony to his own experience when he said, "I was born gay." He then went on to say, "...with the full knowledge and blessing of God!"

The Metropolitan Community Church has now grown into a denomination with congregations in cities across the country. It provides an alternative to persons who feel unwelcome in their own denominations. Although I am heartened by this story, I do not want to leave the Episcopal Church. It is my church of choice, where I feel at home except for this unresolved issue. I speak for many when I say that we do not want to be driven out; we want to be made to feel at home.

Some of us testify that we belong to parishes that fully accept us as we are. They seem to "get" that our condition is natural in the same way that yours is natural. We define natural as the way God made us. We testify to great joy and spiritual strength from being a part of such congregations, although there is usually a minority who make it clear to us that they are displeased that we are there and are accepted openly. After a time, however, the strangeness gives way to familiarity and we just get on with the business of building the kingdom of God.

CHOICES WE FACE ABOUT "COMING OUT"

I would like you to consider with me the choices we face as homosexual persons. As a child I discovered my sexual orientation. I kept it hidden in my subconscious, but by junior high school the reality exploded into my conscious mind and I found myself living with a terrible secret. I had to endure unbelievable social and psychological pressure. As I grew older, nothing wounded me more than being called a "faggot" or "sissy." Away from home, from the prying eyes of my family and my church youth group, I began to tentatively explore this sexual identity. I then began a long struggle that tore apart my inner psyche. I had a driving desire to be accepted and an equally strong desire to rebel. No wonder that 40% of runaway boys are gay. What should I do? What choices do I have as a homosexual person?

I can go through life pretending that I am heterosexual. I learned that was the road taken by most persons in the past and it is the preferred path of my family and my church. Pretend the problem does not exist. Live with it. I can then be a respected, functioning member of society. I sometimes think that I can find a person of the other gender that I like, and perhaps I will grow into a physical attraction for that person. I am aware that in the past many of us married because we saw that alternatives were bleak. Research statistics show that 30% of gay men who acknowledge their sexual orientation have been married or are still married to women.[105] I know that I would be miserable, going through life living a lie, promising in my wedding vows to "love" when my real love lay elsewhere.

Another choice for me is to go through life as a single person. I would hope to be strong in my faith and live a celibate life to the glory of God. I learned at church that the sin of homosexuality is not in my "given" orientation, but rather in actively expressing my sexuality. That, I understand, is also the position of the Roman Catholic Church. And yet, that is a price I do not really want to pay. Celibacy through the ages has been revered in the Church, but it has always been a voluntary choice for one called into special religious orders. I have come to believe that the heterosexual world is unfairly imposing on me a standard the vast majority of them would not accept for themselves. Frankly, I wonder if these people know about the Golden Rule. Living a celibate life is not who I really am. What other choices do I have?

I could decide to live in two worlds at once. In the public arena, whether at church, with family, or on the job, I would pose as straight, but in private I would be myself and have a same-sex relationship. That seems to be the option accepted by society as a way to avoid the issue. The United States military popularized this option with the official policy of "Don't ask, don't tell." It means living a lie, living in the closet with the constant fear of being discovered. I observe many persons like me devise clever ruses to keep folks from guessing their identity. They date persons of the opposite sex. I know two gay men, each of whom lives with a lesbian woman. The two couples take turns visiting at each other's houses. They have dinner and spend the night with their real partners, while they continue to hide their identities in public. I know of variations on this theme that are being played out all across America. This solution permits my kind of person to have a gay or lesbian life on a part-time basis. It has the advantage of sweeping the issue under the rug for the mainstream community.

I find that most of you folks really want to accept us and respect the choices we make in our private lives. You want to let us be ourselves. However, I also notice that many of you are hesitant to speak out in support of gay and lesbian persons because your friends and colleagues are so adamant against us. Rather than confront our opponents with firmness, many of you follow the path of least resistance and remain silent.

Finally, I have the choice of accepting my identity and proclaiming it to the world. I know that my life will be filled with difficulty from that day forward. I will be harassed, reviled, threatened, and even face the possibility of being beaten or killed. But I also know that the only way to change hearts and minds is for us to "come out" and make our case with a wary public. I am heartened to see an ever increasing number of us making our identities known and also demanding our right to be ourselves.

WHAT WE WANT FROM THE CHURCH

What do we, as gay and lesbian persons, want from the church? Our baptismal vow asks each of us to "seek and serve Christ in all persons." Many gay and lesbian church members feel, quite frankly, that the congregation is now prepared to seek God in ethnic minorities, in women, in children, in the poor, but not in that final category, the homosexual person. Yet in some strange way I still have faith in the gospel of Jesus, that the tide will turn and I will find my peace in and through my church.

We feel that so long as a gay or lesbian person cannot attain the rank of bishop, or even presiding bishop, to that extent gay and lesbian persons are not accorded the dignity of full membership. In short, gay and lesbian persons ask the church to remove the stigma, to stop viewing us as "queer." We ask that you accept us as we are, and demand the very same level of accountability, spiritual devotion and leadership qualities from us as from any other church member, priest or bishop.

SAME-GENDER MARRIAGE

We know some of you believe that you are protecting the sanctity of marriage by opposing the right for us to be included. We are not demeaning marriage; quite the contrary. We honor marriage for you and want to strengthen it for all of us. We fail to understand the argument that marriage in America will fall into shambles when we are accorded the same right that you have always enjoyed. We are reminded of words spoken by U.S. Senator Patrick Leahy of Vermont, a practicing Roman Catholic, who was debating the prospect of a constitutional amendment outlawing same-gender marriage. He said, "I have been married for 42 years to the most beautiful woman I have ever known. We don't feel that our marriage is in jeopardy from gays and lesbians and we don't need a constitutional amendment to protect it."

Gay and lesbian persons want to marry and we ask the right to marry the person of our choice. As Christians, we believe that marriage is "an honorable estate." We have been taught by our church to enter marriage asking the blessing of God. Like other members, we seek the support of family, friends, and our church community. Given the level of rejection we face from our foes, we indeed need an additional level of affirmation. We need real support, not rejection or even tolerance. Here we come into the "Body of Christ" asking you to confirm and sanctify our marriages. We come to a body in which "there is neither Jew nor Greek, bonded or free, male or female, for we are all one in Christ Jesus, our Lord."

Some of you ask with exasperation, "Why do you insist on marrying?" We respond quite simply, "For the same reasons that you do." The right of our straight brothers and sisters to marry is a "given" and is accepted without a second thought. Your question "why" would be asked only by those who have never been deprived of this awesome and fulfilling opportunity. To most of us it is more fundamental even than the right to vote.

We want to marry because we are in love with and committed to a person of our choice. Some of you apparently believe that the quality of our love is inferior to your heterosexual love. We don't think so. We remind you that love is not a minor human need. You quote the passage in Genesis that says God created man, and then God created woman and God brought them together as one. But God did more creating. We believe that God created some same-gender persons for each other. We refer you to the scripture in Genesis, also valid for our day, "God saw that it was not good for man to be alone...."

Many of my heterosexual family and friends say that their wedding day was one of the highlights of their lives. It was a time to publicly exchange wedding vows in the presence of family, friends, and often others in the church fellowship. On wedding days parents often acknowledge the passage to adulthood. The community affirms that the single person has become a responsible adult. Who in America would believe they had a right to "the pursuit of happiness" if it did not include the right to marry? We want to share those same benefits and blessings. I testify that the most difficult and depressing days of my life are when I go to the weddings of my heterosexual friends. I wish them all happiness in their loving adventures, but I realize with grief and pain that I may never have the opportunity for a Christian wedding.

Many of us have come to understand that marriage offers the deepest means for our development in relationship. Marriage is the avenue through which we can grow sexually and emotionally. In fact, for many of us marriage is the only way congruent with our Christian values to integrate our physical and moral lives as fully functioning human beings.

Let us face the fact that most of the sexual experience in our subculture has been promiscuous. The larger secular culture has told us that unless we are sexually experimental we are not free. Of course, this message victimizes gays and straights alike, but for us there has been no "pot of gold at the end of the rainbow" or social incentive to rein in our impulses. Many of us treat sex as central to our lives. In defense, you cannot know what it feels like to have your sexual identity smudged out from birth, to have your sexual desires considered the worst kind of depravity, or to have your yearnings for love defined as unspeakable vice. All of these feelings are in the background as we approach the sexual experience.

The sober realization has dawned on most of us that living promiscuously has been one cause of the spread of AIDS. Some of us have AIDS, and are living on borrowed time. All of us have friends and perhaps lovers who have died in this epidemic. Many who were promiscuous in the past have moved away from casual sex. We want to live in committed and permanent relationships so that AIDS can recede into the background of our daily reality. Public acceptance of open, committed same-sex relationships would be an enormous support for this trend in our community. As Christians, we further appreciate the value of marriage as a deeper sanctification of our committed partnerships, and we want this in our lives. We hope that our call appeals to the most conservative among you who believe in marriage and the importance of discipline in the marriage vows.

HIV/AIDS AND THE GAY COMMUNITY
Those of us who were adults in the late 1980's and the early 1990's remember most vividly making and honoring the AIDS quilts which were brought to the nation's capitol from across the country. Many of the quilts were displayed on the walls of our church sanctuaries and in the undercrofts in churches across Washington, D.C. At the time of the first demonstration in 1987, there were a few thousand quilts and most of

us who carried them to the mall were from the gay and lesbian community.

A few years later there was a second batch of quilts on display and another demonstration. On this occasion tapestry filled the ellipse, with each quilt composed of many blocks, each block representing a life and death due to AIDS. We noted that probably half of the much larger crowd of demonstrators was straight. More people were marching in sympathy for us, but also the AIDS epidemic was growing to include an ever larger number of heterosexual persons.

A final quilt demonstration was held in 1996. So many more had died. It was an amazing sight. Quilts were spread from the Washington monument to the steps of the Capitol. Tens of thousands of people congregated. A deep hush fell over the vast throng of demonstrators in the face of overwhelming tragedy and death represented in these quilts.

Some of the quilt pieces were identified by full names, others only by first names, and yet others by nicknames. Parents, siblings, and lovers had made panels. One, for example, said, "My precious son and best friend." Some panels were tacky and others were elegant. The variety of themes, images and materials added to their vitality. We felt that each panel spoke in its own language to a great global tragedy that had to be brought under control, as we paid homage to the dead. We listened as the names were read. On and on the reading went, hour after hour. In that day of anguish, many of us heard the call to promote marriage as an alternative to chaos and death.[106]

We are saddened to report a drug of choice that is becoming popular among gays. Crystal methamphetamine, known as speed, is a mood elevator and a fatigue reducer. It is a powerful sexual stimulant that reduces inhibitions, bolsters confidence and heightens the intensity of sexual experience. Furthermore, the drug is inexpensive and readily available. It is also addictive when used to excess and quickly destroys one's health.

The epidemic of HIV is again growing rapidly among this group of users, estimated to affect ten percent of the gay population. Men in their forties who thought they were dying but found new life with drug treatment are using speed. Most of them throw caution to the wind, often having multiple sex partners on a single night, abandoning protection from infection. Too many men who are not infected say they feel guilty for not having AIDS.

The Church can view this new development in one of two ways. One is to understand these men as irresponsible hedonists who live for today's pleasure with no thought for tomorrow. The other perspective is to see them as men who are lonely and depressed. They have low self-esteem because of their rejection by society. Likewise, they have no sense of permanence or stability in their sexual relations. At least partly because of these conditions, they are making foolish choices and destroying their lives.

THANK YOU FOR STANDING WITH US

In closing, we wish to express our profound gratitude to the Episcopal Church. Most persons in our community have long since given up on the church, considering it a hostile environment. Many ask those of us in the church why we want to associate with such a regressive institution. But those of us who have been "born of water and the Spirit," those who call Jesus "Lord" want desperately to deal with the issues we have raised. We want to help in healing this long-established rupture in the body of Christ.

Your vote at General Convention in Minneapolis to support the election and consecration of the Rev. V. Gene Robinson as Bishop of New Hampshire gave us new reason for hope. It gave us, further, a way to confront those in the gay and lesbian movement who believe not only that the church is irrelevant but also that it is an obstacle, a negative force, in the battle for justice. Many of my friends have nothing but disdain for traditional churches. They feel that those who guard the gates do so as prejudiced persons, determined to keep us from entering.

We, therefore, recognize with great appreciation that the Episcopal Church in the United States stood with us recently against the pressures of many in the world Anglican Communion and the dissent of other fellow Episcopalians. We know that you struggled hard and understood fully the implication of your stand. Further, we express gratitude for the clear, unambiguous stand of the United Church of Christ. There are other Christian bodies in this country and around the world who have adopted positions that recognize us as entitled to the full acceptance of church and society. We shall be grateful always in what we believe is a true expression of the church at its best, standing against the many honest constituents who disagree, as well as against a thoughtless world. Thank you.

Chapter 10
A CASE FOR SAME-GENDER MARRIAGE

> Let each of you lead the life that the Lord has
> assigned, to which God called you. This is my
> rule in all the churches.
> —I Corinthians 7:17

Delegate Adam P. Ebbin, a gay state legislator
in Virginia, spoke against passage of a Constitutional
Amendment to exclude same-gender civil or religious
unions. He spoke also against other legislative proposals
that would prevent same-gender couples from jointly
owning property or receiving any benefits that normally
accrue to married couples. "We are about to write
discrimination into our State Constitution and we are
about to exclude gays and lesbians from mainstream
society," he said.

Delegate Ebbin then responded to "the gentle
lady from Campbell County" who had stated that the
constitutional amendment would protect the institution
of marriage. He asked how many members of the
legislature were divorced. He then wanted to know how
many had children, or parents, or brothers, or sisters who
are divorced. He wanted to know what gays and lesbians
have to do with the divorces of the delegates or their
families. He then asked how many of those marriages
were celebrated in a church or synagogue. "Why are you
blaming same-gender couples for the fact that you have
broken vows to God and your spouses?" He continued,

"I will not stand by while this body uses gays and lesbians as scapegoats for what has happened to the institution of marriage." Mr. Ebbin closed has remarks by saying rational Virginians have nothing to fear from gays and lesbians. There is no threat to the institution of marriage from loving, committed same-gender couples.

The people of Massachusetts have reached that conclusion. In mid-September 2005 the House and Senate met jointly and voted down a proposed constitutional amendment that would have eliminated same-sex marriage, legalized two years earlier, and replaced it with "civil unions" for gay couples. The vote was 157 to 39. Commentators credit the ordinariness of the weddings with diffusing some of the opposition. Sixty one hundred couples have married since November 2003 when the Supreme Court ruled in favor of seven same-gender couples who had petitioned for the right to marry. The court concluded that "the right to marry means little if it does not include the right to marry the person of one's choice." People realize from observation that there is no threat to the institution of marriage. Each of the marriages made it more ordinary and helped overcome the shock of something new.

What are the claims of those who seek passionately to preserve marriage for a man and a woman? What counter-claims are offered by those who wish to promote a new understanding of marriage that includes same-gender unions? What is it that makes marriage sacred? Is it appropriate for the Episcopal Church and other denominations to bless same-gender unions? Should such blessing take the form of holy matrimony?

Most of the arguments against same-gender unions or marriages can be summarized under three headings:

- God created marriage between man and woman in the Garden of Eden. Monogamous marriage between man and woman has remained unchanged from the beginning of time until now.
- Man and woman were created for each other. Written into human nature is the principle of complementarity. Their bodies and psychological natures were meant for each other. That is the eternal order that God created. Men are created to lead, to protect and to make final decisions as head of the household. Women are created to be helpmates, to bear and nurture children, and to support the life and work of the man.
- Marriage is meant for procreation, which obviously is inconsistent with homosexuality. The open practice of homosexuality is leading to the breakdown of marriage by creating confusion about the proper roles of men and women. People need to stop exploring new fads and get back to living by eternal verities.

Let us examine each of these claims.

MARRIAGE IN THE BIBLE

Two United States Senators declared on the floor of that august chamber when the debate was raging over a constitutional amendment to limit marriage to a union between one man and one woman that the institution of marriage they wanted to preserve goes back all the way through biblical history to the Garden of Eden. One Republican and one Democrat saw their vote for a constitutional amendment as a defense of marriage as God created it.

The actual practice of marriage developed differently. The only people who can say that marriage has always been between "one man and one woman" are ones who have never studied the text of the Bible, much less world cultural history. Polygamy was a common form of marriage in the Bible, as was keeping one or more concubines, who were usually slaves. Abraham had at least one concubine from whom many descendants claim their heritage. Abraham's son Isaac prospered and had a "great household."[107] His two sons, Esau and Jacob had multiple wives and concubines. Jacob was married to Leah and Rachael but he also had children by their maids.[108] Esau was angry that his father had arranged for Jacob to get wives from his mother's family, so he did the same, although he already had wives.[109]

It is clear that Hebrew society, especially among the more affluent, did not generally practice monogamy. We need look no further than the Ten Commandments to get a sense of the marital structure of society. "You shall not covet your neighbor's house; you shall not covet your neighbor's wife, or male or female slave, or ox, or donkey, or anything that belongs to your neighbor."[110] Female slaves or concubines were the property of men, who thereby had sexual rights over them.

In the era of the Kings of Israel, David had many wives and concubines, yet he was described as a man after God's own heart.[111] Solomon's reign was one of splendor, as evidenced by the large number of his wives.

Solomon took wives to seal alliances with foreign powers, as when he made a marriage alliance with Pharaoh, King of Egypt. Solomon's wisdom, his opulence, and his large happy family awed the Queen of Sheba when she came on a State visit. She noted, "Happy are your wives."[112] Solomon's wives included "seven hundred princesses and three hundred concubines."[113]

Hebrew culture assumed that multiple wives were appropriate, and that the taking concubines was a normal practice. Naturally, kings should enjoy the fruits of their position by having many wives. It is probable that most poor men had only one wife. It is also evident from a careful study of the Old Testament that after the exile and the writing of the Leviticus Code monogamy became the more accepted pattern for marital relations.

It is interesting to compare a wedding in ancient Israel with our weddings. In biblical times there was no religious ceremony connected with the wedding. The essence of the wedding was the removal of the bride from her father's house to that of the bridegroom or his father's house. The father of the groom or a male member of his family chose the bride, came to her house and made arrangements, including a dowry given to the family of the bride. It was agreed that on a certain day and hour the bridegroom would come and take his bride. His friends usually accompanied the groom when he came for her. She had bathed, dressed, and was waiting anxiously for his arrival. Back at the residence where they would live, a party had been planned with neighbors, family and friends.[114] A feast followed; indeed there were festivities for seven to fourteen days.[115]

On some occasions there was an oath or a pledge,[116] and on other occasions someone gave a blessing to the couple.[117] At the end of the evening, the bride was conducted to her chamber where a canopy had been prepared.[118] The groom was exempt from military service for one year in order to spend time with his bride.[119]

We now turn to the story of Adam and Eve. The creation story in Genesis has immense importance. Here was expressed the ideal of man and woman created for each other, the two becoming "one flesh." This story points to a holy gift from God. It suggests that God's ideal intention for heterosexual persons is monogamy in a life-long relationship between a man and a woman. The creation account also emphasizes procreation, so the human family could "multiply and replenish the earth."

There were at least four accounts of creation told around countless campfires on the Judean hills over centuries of time. The authors of Genesis brought them together in a single account, probably written in final form at the end of the Babylonian Captivity. The stories point to a high standard and provide us with the ideal of mutual love and fulfillment within the bonds of matrimony. The Genesis account of creation also offers the most profound insight into God's creative power and the birth of humanity as a special delight, because of God's loving nature.

Yet married life during the Old Testament era was far from ideal from a woman's perspective. Her status was inferior to that of her husband. When she married, it was usually without her consent. She was transferred from the control of her father to live under the authority of her husband. Usually, there was a "bride price" paid by the family of the groom to the family of the bride. While this was not perceived strictly as a purchase, it did emphasize that she was then the possession of her husband.

The practice of divorce was widespread. When the husband was no longer satisfied with his wife or found her to be offensive in some way, he would write out a document of divorce and send her away. But where would she go? She was disgraced for not being a virgin, and often she found it difficult to find another acceptable marriage partner. And where could she find employment if she were a single woman? If she were childless at her husband's death, by levirate law she was given in marriage to her deceased husband's brother, although he was already married. If there were no brother, the widow was left destitute and often became a beggar or prostitute to survive. At the same time, the wife had no legal right to divorce her husband, no matter how cruelly she was treated.

Feminists point out that the creation account described a sexist society, and puts a theological stamp on what for us is an unjust cultural pattern. First in the creation account, Adam is lonesome without a helpmate, so God takes one of his ribs and creates woman. She was created as a helpmate for Adam, not primarily the two for each other. The story of disobedience and fall in the Garden of Eden depicts Eve as falling prey to temptation and eating the fruit, then tempting Adam and causing him to disobey as well. The story suggests that the pain in childbirth is just punishment for Eve's sin. In all of these accounts there is a subtle, perhaps unconscious depiction of women as inferior to men, placing on their shoulders the burden for sin coming into the world, and hence leading them to feel a special guilt.

The cultural drive for large families was so strong that a woman who could not bear children was often treated as an outcast. She could be divorced, or the man could take one or more concubines in order to produce his children.

This rather lengthy account of wedding practices, multiple wives, inferior women's status and divorce was an evolutionary process that led toward monogamy in the centuries before Jesus. There was no single pattern of marriage back through the centuries to the beginning of time.

At the conclusion of the Anglican marriage ceremony, the priest uses the words of Jesus and declares, "What God has joined together, let no man put asunder." Or, in the Revised Standard Version, "What God has joined together, let no one separate."[120]

Jesus spoke these words while debating a Pharisee who came to ask him about whether it is lawful for a man to divorce his wife. Jesus quickly elevated the issue to the larger question of the meaning of marriage and justice for women. Jesus responded in his customary way by asking the inquirer to look behind the Law of Moses, which established the legal rules for divorce. He declared that God instituted marriage in the creation of humanity. God has always willed a permanent union of a man and a woman. Jesus quoted Genesis 2:24: "For this reason a man shall leave his father and mother and be joined to his wife and the two shall be one flesh."[121]

PAUL AND THE EARLY CHURCH ADAPT TO LOCAL CULTURES

The Apostle Paul made a strategic decision when he provided practical guidance for the churches on all kinds of cultural matters. He advised the flock to obey Christ within existing structures rather than a more radical approach that would challenge the structures of most cultural institutions. The glaring exception to this generalization was Paul's agreement with Peter on not requiring Gentiles to practice Jewish law. Notice how Paul accepted the institution of slavery, of male dominance in the church and of customs about women wearing long hair and of covering themselves. All of these things were by deliberate choice as Paul noted in the scripture quoted at the beginning of this chapter. "Let each of you lead the life that the Lord has assigned, to which God called you. This is my rule in all the churches." Paul could have insisted on a radical reading of Jesus words. He acknowledged them in principle when he said, "In Christ there is neither Jew nor Greek, bond or free, male or female, for we are all one in Christ."

If we take Paul seriously in this policy, and if we concede that homosexuality is a given and not a life-style choice, we conclude that these persons should lead the homosexual life that the Lord has assigned. Upon reflection, we further conclude that excluding homosexual persons is not in line with his great principle that we are all one in Christ. Paul was struggling to give sound if confusing advice to the church at Corinth. He was trying to be true to the mind of Christ, yet confessing that in some specific situations he was merely giving his own opinion, while dealing with practical situations in a Gentile society.

In the instructive chapter of I Corinthians Paul said in regard to marital lifestyles, "each of you has a particular gift from God." Paul never understood homosexuality as a gift from God. He saw it only in its promiscuous or abusive form. But his principle goes to the heart of the wisdom of accepting gays and lesbians into the fellowship of Christ. "…but each has a particular gift from God, one having one kind and another having a different kind…."[122] The Episcopal Church, among others, now proclaims that some bring the gift of homosexuality. Let it be accepted, honored, controlled responsibly, and used as a gift from God.

Many people in the church, both scholars and laity, both men and women, but especially women, express their anger and frustration at the Apostle Paul for his attitude toward women and later for his apparent attitude toward homosexuality. We counsel patience with Paul, reminding parishioners of his extraordinary brilliant and helpful theology that connected the Christ events to the larger Greek/Roman world. His faltering on dealing with embedded customs must be placed in the context of having to deal with a Gentile society and its pagan background, when the Christian community was small and in a precarious situation. He may have felt, as a practical matter, that his hearers could not absorb his high demands for personal morality and at the same time deal with changing social structures. Consider how slow we are coming to grips with homosexuality in the church, and one appreciates the dilemma faced by the great Apostle. Yet, his failure to deal fully with the implications of Jesus' love ethic has left that task to us, some two thousand years later.

The point of this lengthy discussion is to refute the notion that marriage has been unchanged through the ages, as given by God in the Garden of Eden. Marriage has evolved through the ages. In our tradition it has become more centered in the love ethic of Jesus. The acceptance of homosexual persons as marriage partners is another important step in this evolution.

MAN AND WOMAN COMPLEMENT EACH OTHER

The second reason persons oppose same-gender relationships is the complementary relationship between male and female. After all, the obvious fact is that human procreation comes from the physical sexual act, requiring both the male and female bodies. These same persons point to a possible psychic complementary relationship as well. The male appears to be stronger and more aggressive; the female needs more protection and also is more protective of the child who is vulnerable.

When God created heterosexual persons, God made man and woman for each other. Let us all rejoice in that wonderful gift from heaven. But we need not be blinded to God's having also created some with an affinity for persons of the same-gender. The simple question is whether we can make room for such diversity in the creativity of God.

Dr. H. Richard Niebuhr, Professor of Christian Ethics at Yale University Divinity School, would say often that we are usually right in what we affirm and wrong in what we deny. In this instance that army of Christian soldiers who wish to affirm the sanctity of marriage between a man and woman is correct. Marriage is sacred and it is complementary. The position taken by those who affirm homosexuality is also correct, although denied by that other army of saints. Same-gender marriage is natural and proper for persons whose physical and emotional attraction is to each other. It is most improper to force a union that is unnatural. So the traditionalists affirm what they know to be true, but deny what others of us also know to be true. Heterosexual marriage is normal and appropriate for most people. But it is not "normative," as something to be emulated by everyone.

MARRIAGE AND PROCREATION

The third argument made by those who wish to preserve marriage for heterosexual couples is that marriage is meant primarily for the procreation of children, or at least marriage should have the potential for children, with their attendant nurture to maturity. That was the view held by our own Church historically and is the official position of the Roman Catholic Church to this day.

The Anglican Church revised its doctrines about marriage as well as the liturgy of marriage after the break with Rome. The Prayer Book of 1552 stated that the purposes of marriage are: (1) making sacred the union between a man and a woman, (2) the procreation of children, (3) and the mutual sharing for the benefit of both. We note that this third statement is an addition to the Roman view.

Now let us notice briefly the current liturgy for *The Celebration and Blessing of a Marriage*.[123] The

Celebrant states the sacredness of the union, namely, it is in the presence of God that we witness and bless this union. She or he notes that God established marriage in creation. Our Lord performed his first miracle at a wedding. Further, marriage signifies the mystery of the union between Christ and the Church.

Note the evolution from earlier ceremonies, "The union of husband and wife in heart, body and mind is intended by God for their mutual joy." "Help and comfort" is moved to second place, and in third place, "And when it is God's will, for the procreation of children and their nurture in the knowledge and love of the Lord."

The early **Book of Common Prayer** provided for the bride to be given by her father to her husband, a carryover from early Hebrew history when the woman was almost considered as property. The old ceremony provided for giving and receiving a single ring, again symbolizing the possession of her as property held by the man. The early ceremony also used the words, "man and wife" reflecting the assumption that the man maintained his status while the woman lost her identity as an individual. These elements reflect assumptions common to the sixteenth century, when the early liturgy was written.

Notice the charge which acknowledges the necessity of meeting legal requirements as well as religious obligations. The ceremony now requires the free consent of both parties. The declaration covenant is now exactly the same for both the man and the woman.

So, marriage for Episcopalians has evolved to express a wedding ceremony that reflects the equality of the partners in a relationship of mutuality. It does not require intended procreation as the primary rationale for marriage, and it does require the free consent of both parties. What an evolution! Our considered conclusion is that the decision by the Episcopal Church and most other mainline Protestant denominations to honor women and men as equals in marriage has led to the logical conclusion that women are worthy of ordination into the priesthood. All evidence points to the belief that this same attitude of respect for the dignity of every person forms the basis for inclusion of homosexual persons into the church.

While the Episcopal wedding ceremony states first that marriage is intended for the couple's mutual joy and fulfillment, in contrast, the Roman Catholic position on the purpose of marriage is mired in the theology of the middle ages. Recently a spokesman for the bishops of Spain agreed to permit the use of condoms to prevent AIDS in Africa. The next day the bishops issued a statement retracting the one of the previous day. It stated again the Vatican prohibition on the use of contraceptives. The statement explained, "Condom use implies immoral sexual conduct." The church supports only "faithful conjugal love." It further explained the Church's position, even within marriage. "Each and every marital act must of necessity retain its intrinsic relation to the procreation of children."[124]

In the 1995 "Evangelism Vitae" or "Gospel of Life" document, the pontiff lumped contraception even in marriage with abortion and euthanasia. The document condemned "a civilization of affluence and pleasure as though sin did not exist and God did not exist."

We return to the observation that negative attitudes

toward lesbians and gays are almost always correlated with second-class status of women. If men are meant to dominate women, that symbol cannot be expressed in same-gender relations and therefore it must be rejected.

Look carefully at a recent story in the **New York Times**. The title was "Clerics Fighting a Gay Festival for Jerusalem." Religious leaders representing traditional elements within Christianity, Judaism and Islam came together for a news conference to denounce a gay festival planned for Jerusalem. It was noted that although they agree on almost nothing, this issue created strong bonds of unity. There was the Muslim Sheik, the Latin Patriach, the Armenian Archbishop, and the Ashkenazi Chief Rabbi. Of course, there was also the Evangelical preacher from the United States who came to Jerusalem to organize and incite the group. Abdel Aziz Bukhari, a Sufi sheik stated, "We can't permit anybody to come and make the holy city dirty. This is very ugly and very nasty to have these people come to Jerusalem." Another leader agreed. "We are a holy city not a homo city."[125]

When one takes the time to get acquainted with these faith traditions one notices immediately that they all hold women in positions of inferiority to men. It will be difficult for them to accept same-gender unions or marriages when their own views on equality of the sexes are so tied to another age.

Few if any of us believe that marriage is improper apart from procreation. We do not deny marriage to a couple who know they cannot bear children. The marriage and remarriage of older persons in our society have lead many to find happiness, companionship and security in their later years. The purpose of their marriage is noble but it does not include procreation.

Same-gender marriage can be holy with its own grand purposes without including the procreation of children. Indeed, one can argue that in this era when the greater good is not procreation to replenish the earth, but rather restraint to alleviate the overpopulation of the earth, same-gender marriages fulfill a privileged place in God's design.

The argument is made that children adopted by same-gender couples receive inherently inferior care because a child needs the role models provided by both a man and a woman. Research studies and observation by the American Psychological Association lead us to believe that many same-gender couples do remarkable jobs in producing well-rounded children. A report in *Pediatrics* pronounced that "a growing body of scientific literature demonstrates that children who grow up with one or two gay and/or lesbian parents fare as well in emotional, cognitive, social, and sexual functioning as do children whose parents are heterosexual."[126] Opponents claim the research studies are flawed and objective researchers admit that it is difficult to do scientific sampling. The key factors are security, love and discipline. Without claiming too much, the evidence is overwhelming that two caring persons of the same sex can provide more stability than a single-mother or father raising a child alone. Of course, the results depend on the particular qualities of the parent. Certainly, loving same-gender couples provide more support than do bitter and tension-filled heterosexual parents. We must be careful about making sweeping pronouncements on who is best qualified as parents.

There are differences between men and women. It does not serve the common good to ignore such differences. Much of the research on disease and treatment of illness has historically used males for the studies and as a result the medical decisions often have favored men to the disadvantage of women. There can be complementarity between the sexes without conceding inequality. The disadvantage suffered by women in the workplace because they bear the children can be mitigated by enlightened employment policies, but never completely overcome.

The basic point is that we have outgrown the era of male dominance over women. We respect equality. We honor it and are ready to defend it with all of our being. We believe God does not discriminate in regard to gender. We invite all churches and cultural subgroups to join us in the age of equality because it is the right thing to do. This is relevant to the topic we are considering, because when we respect women as equal to men, we are then led to respect same-gender relationships that fulfill the physical and psychic needs of the individuals involved.

ELEMENTS OF A CHRISTIAN MARRIAGE

The key issues are not procreation and complementarity. The qualities that support a Christian marriage are love, loyalty, caring, cooperation and responsibility. It is placing God at the center of life. Sexual compatibility is always a significant consideration. Marriage is about mutual affection and therefore it is about the right to choose ones partner.

The issues surrounding marriage are indeed serious. They deserve the focused attention of the church. Some use homosexuality as a metaphor for what they see as the collapsing morality around marriage. They feel a need to hold the line. Rather than place emphasis on underlying causes of the breakdown of marriage, they assume that all of those ills are in some way linked to acceptance of responsible homosexuality. All factions in the great cultural debate would be well served to join hands and hearts in evaluating causes for the breakdown in marriage and then working jointly to deal with them. We can all agree that there is much work to do to stabilize and enhance marriage.

We do not agree that recognition and support for same-gender unions or marriage is evidence of a breakdown in morality. Rather, the encouragement of life-long commitments for same-gender couples moves society away from random and promiscuous behavior toward stable lives and real intimacy. By not recognizing the legitimacy of same-gender marriage, we encourage unequally yoked couples into heterosexual marriages with all of the unintended destructive consequences.

ESSENTIAL ELEMENTS IN A CHRISTIAN MARRIAGE

Let us turn now to consider in more detail the elements essential for a Christian marriage. We take a step back from the immediate consideration of whom one should marry and consider the qualities that are important in a good marriage.[127]

First, marriage is a commitment between two consenting adults. Such persons affirm their love for each other and resolve to commit themselves to permanently support each other. They recognize that dark days will come as well as those filled with sunshine. They thus repeat "for better for worse, for richer for poorer, in sickness and in health…." Gay and lesbian persons ask for the right to choose their partners based on love and attraction so they can make this commitment.

Second, marriage is more than a surface and momentary infatuation. It should also be based on a more fundamental compatibility. Those who champion union between a man and a woman rightly make that argument. But what if the compatibility does not exist with persons of the opposite gender? What if the compatibility is found with a person of the same gender? Would it be a Christian marriage if the two persons were forced into a pattern that misrepresented their essential natures? Alternately, should gays and lesbians be asked to live celibate lives, denying them the loving relationship that helps to fulfill life?

Third, marriage is more than a piece of paper in the form of a license, and more than a commitment based on good intentions. Marriage is a legal agreement as part of the structure of civil life. Marriage confers hundreds of federal benefits and privileges based on laws and regulatory rulings. Marriage is about entitlements. Those who are barred from these entitlements, which they want and need, are left isolated and bereft of societal largess.

Dietrich Bonhoeffer wrote in 1943 from his Nazi prison cell to a young bride and groom. "Your love is your own private possession. But marriage is more than something personal—it is a status, an office. Just as it is the crown, and not merely the will to rule, that makes the king, so it is marriage, and not merely your love for each other, that joins you together in the sight of God and man...." He went on to conclude, "It is not your love that sustains the marriage, but from now on, the marriage that sustains your love."

Marriage is a status to which couples graduate. It defines commitment, intention and legal responsibility. Love and law become intertwined. Can Christians ask same-gender couples to forego the spiritual, legal and civil rewards of life together, which are so integral to personal and societal fulfillment? Can society demand a level of responsibility from homosexual couples that it does not ask of others?

MARRIAGE OR CIVIL UNION?

Finally, we face the issue of whether same-gender commitments should be "unions" or marriages. We begin by the assertion that they should be unions by whatever name. The state has an obligation to treat all citizens with equal justice. There is always a distinction, even in church-related marriages, between the role of the church and that of the state. The ceremony may be religious, but the marriage license is issued by the state, which confers upon the clergy the right to act as representative of the state for the purpose of conducting the wedding ceremony.

At issue within the Church is the question of whether such commitments should be considered as marriage or simply "union." Some of us in the church see the latter as a reasonable compromise. After all, marriage has always been between a man and a woman. Out of respect for ancient traditions and what many feel is a scriptural basis, they feel more comfortable with such a distinction. Given the deep division within the Church, this may be a reasonable accommodation. Certainly such a compromise would be a sure step forward in the long struggle for acceptance by same-gender persons. Most gay and lesbian persons and others of us who wish to stand in solidarity with them would agree that a partial victory is better than total defeat.

However, there is a strong case to be made for marriage. We remind ourselves that the Church as the Body of Christ is commissioned to mediate the grace of God through marriage. The Episcopal Church has never considered marriage to be a sacrament, as does the Roman Catholic Church. We have only two sacraments; namely, Baptism and Eucharist. However, we recognize that marriage can have sacramental qualities. Do we want to bestow the full blessing of God by recognizing the union as marriage?

The gay or lesbian couple comes to the office of the rector for counseling. They are active communicants, bound by the Lordship of Christ. They declare their love for each other and ask their rector to preside at a wedding ceremony. The rector is aware of "fruits of the Spirit"— gentleness, kindness, qualities present in their lives, and discerns a holiness, a place that welcomes God. Does the rector bestow the full dignity and worth of the Church on this homosexual couple? She can turn them away, she can offer the blessing of a union, or she can marry them. Most likely that decision will be determined not by the rector in her office but by the national church at General Convention.

Some of us would argue that talk about "gay

marriage" misses the point. Let us talk about marriage, its meaning and purpose, and what happens when it is solemnized. It is about love. It is about family values. It is about commitment. It is about gaining the support of family and the larger society for the union. It is about dedicating the union to God.

In closing, step back and consider a new definition of marriage for us in the church. The definition is a summary of the case that has been presented in this chapter, and indeed, in this book.

A Christian marriage is a partnership based on mutual affection between two adults of equal legal and moral standing. It is reserved for those who confess their faith and seek to live under the Lordship of Christ. Marriage is freely bestowed by the Church, acting as God's agent, upon those who choose to accept its duties and responsibilities. The underlying purpose of marriage is to protect and encourage the union of committed couples and to confirm their rights and responsibilities to society. The qualities that support a Christian marriage are love, loyalty, caring, cooperation and responsibility— all with God at the center of the home.

Chapter 11
LETTER TO THE ANGLICAN COMMUNION

> I still have many things to say to you but you
> cannot bear them now. When the Spirit of
> Truth comes, he will guide you into all the
> truth.
> —John 16:12, 13

The ***Windsor Report***, which you published in
2004, expressed dismay that the Episcopal Church in
the United States had consecrated a divorced and openly
gay priest as a bishop. Many of you in the Communion
felt that the Americans had acted hastily, without proper
consultation. You said we did not make a sincere effort to
explain the action, nor did we allow the time necessary
to build consensus. Those who opposed the acceptance
of homosexual persons in church leadership roles asked
for extensive theological and scriptural documentation
to support the practice. In short, the Report asked the
American Church to "make its case." In the meanwhile,
the Anglican Consultative Council asked the American
and Canadian Churches to withdraw from official
representation.

Explanations for the consecration of Bishop
Robinson were presented after the fact but these were
rejected as being insufficient. The claim was that the US
Church argued from secular data, human rights and social
justice grounds rather than from theology and the Bible.
This book is a statement of our case. It is NOT an official

reply; **To Set Our Hope on Christ** is the official response to the Windsor Report. Ours is another prayerful voice that seeks to respond to these legitimate concerns.

In addition to confronting the churches in the United States and Canada, the Windsor Report raised the larger issue of how the worldwide Anglican Communion should deal with internal controversy and how much control might be ceded to central bodies. It is worth noting that no Primate, or leader of a national church, has ever ceded any legal authority to the Archbishop of Canterbury or any centralized ecclesiastical body. It is widely reported within the American Church and in the press that the Archbishop of Canterbury, Rowan Williams, is under intense pressure to crack down on the U.S. and Canadian Churches. Conservative groups within the United States have teamed with African leaders who represent countries and churches where homosexuality is rejected. They are accused of trying to enforce a power play against the Episcopal Church to punish it for the stand that was taken.

For his part, Presiding Bishop, Frank T. Griswold, repeated in a news conference with BBC what he apparently told Anglican leaders at a meeting in Northern Ireland that the US Church "sought to act with integrity" and that the support for Bishop Robinson had been "right and proper." Therefore, he believed, the Church would not retract its decision.

The Episcopal Church is fully supportive of the traditional cooperative relationships with other bodies within the Anglican Communion. There is no desire to "go it alone." As noted in the Windsor Report, we are aware of the proper goal of unity of spirit as part of the one body of Christ. We feel sustained, as do others, by our common liturgical life rooted in the traditions of the Books of Common Prayer. We participate gladly in "the web of relationships with companion dioceses," and in the myriad activities which continue to flourish.

The Report rightly points out how we have stood together in mutual love and service in opposition to racial enslavement and genocide. We have reached out and offered aid in times of famine, disease and chaos. In significant ways, "Anglicans have shared these gifts of communion for the building up of the whole and thereby for the advancement of God's mission."[128]

There are, of course, deep divisions within the American Church and indeed within individual parishes, as in the larger Communion. As an example, at Christ Church, Alexandria, Virginia, Mr. Russell Randle expressed principled opposition to Convention action. He served as a lay deputy to General Convention and is a leader in the Diocese of Virginia. He also led the parish in support of the persecuted church in Sudan, where he has visited, and for whom he has raised significant amounts of money. Mr. Randle grieves for the two million persons of Sudan who died, many for their faith. He feels that the stand of our Church on the election and consecration of Bishop Robinson is driving a wedge between the Church in Africa and ours at a time when we need to support them, and indeed, when we need the refreshing and life-giving active faith of the African Christians. Mr. Randle also recognizes that we need the lost revenue for missions, withheld by dissidents, since General Convention in 2003. He proposes a "gentle toleration" within the United States Church without an endorsement of the gay and lesbian lifestyle. Mr. Randle represents a principled minority in the Church who place the fellowship and joint mission of the worldwide Communion above the value of addressing the issue of homosexuality.

The U.S. Church, while grieving at the break in fellowship and recognizing our lack of sufficient consultation, disagrees with Mr. Randle and others on what is at stake for the long-term integrity of the Church. We do not take our stand to be arbitrary or a cultural fad. We believe deeply that ours is a stand for justice and respect for the dignity of every person. We believe the God who is Father of Jesus the Christ is calling us in our day to a new recognition of his equal love for all people. We believe Jesus issues the invitation for those treated as outcasts to enter the Kingdom of God.

The Episcopal Church especially takes issue with the Reverend Canon David C. Anderson, President and CEO of the American Anglican Council, the leading opposition organization, when he wrote, "The Episcopal Church has declared war on the Anglican Communion because it thinks it knows best and has most of the money. The only thing dropping faster than membership in the Episcopal Church is its global relevancy."[129]

A positive perspective tinged by humor is found in a story told by Bishop Bennett J. Sims, who had been asked to speak at the Baltimore, Maryland Cathedral and later to lead a discussion. The 35 persons who came formed a circle. Bishop Sims asked participants to take a minute and tell about themselves by answering two questions: (1) Are you a lifelong Episcopalian, and (2) What do you like about the Episcopal Church. The man on his right was last to speak. Bishop Sims noted that he had been writing in a small notebook while others were speaking. When it came his turn, he gave his name and then recited the limerick he had just written:

"There was once a Catholic named J
Who found at age three that he was gay.
Long hours in confession
Brought an awful depression
'Till the Anglicans said, 'Okay.'"

A strong feeling of accomplishment and an opportunity for evangelism were expressed at the conclusion of the General Convention in Minneapolis by The Very Rev. George Werner, reelected as president of the House of Deputies. He said, "This Sunday may be one of the greatest if not the best missionary Sunday in the history of the Church." The Church now has a much stronger voice when it invites lesbian and gay persons as well as those who believe the role of the church is to proclaim justice. This is borne out by the testimony of deputies wearing their convention badges on the streets of Minneapolis. CNN television had covered convention proceedings for four hours per day. People on the streets hailed deputies to say they now saw the church in a positive new light. They wanted to say, "Thank you."

THE FIRST WOMAN PRIEST
We accept the invitation to retrace the history of our cooperative relationship and review the ways we have resolved differences in the past. We begin with The Rev. Li Tim Oi, the first woman ever ordained in the Anglican

Church. The Rt. Rev. Ronald Hall, Bishop of Hong Kong and Macau, in 1941 found much of mainland China occupied by the Japanese with Anglican Churches closed. However, the Portuguese colony of Macau was neutral. Refugees, including many Anglicans, flooded into the colony.

Li Tim Oi was named "beloved one" by her father who was grateful to have a baby daughter in a male oriented society. At her baptism she also took the name Florence in memory of Florence Nightingale. She attended a Hong Kong Cathedral service in 1931 at age 23 when a woman was consecrated as a deacon and when the bishop suggested that more women should step up to assume leadership roles in the Church. Li Tim Oi said she felt the bishop was speaking directly to her and so she began a ten year pilgrimage of study and spiritual discernment, including a four year course at a theological school in Canton. In 1941 she was made a deacon.

At Bishop Hall's direction she went to Macau where she was charged with the pastoral care of refugees, which she discharged with grace and compassion. Bishop Hall began making plans to ordain Li Tim Oi when it became evident that neither the bishop nor any other priest could travel to Macau to administer the sacraments. He discussed the matter with his Lutheran friend Rheinhold Niebuhr, when the famed theologian was in Hong Kong. The two agreed that with the war raging the only practical way forward was to ordain her and deal with protocol later. However, it was not until 1944 that Bishop Hall was able to meet her secretly in Guandong Province in unoccupied China. There in the town of Hsinxing at the Anglican Church Bishop Hall lay hands on her in a sacred ceremony and she became the first female priest in the Anglican Church.

They spoke only of the meaning of priesthood and her lifelong commitment, but both were acutely aware that they were breaking with tradition. They felt justified in their actions because the foremost need was for refugees to receive the sacraments and have the ministries of a priest.

The ordination was largely ignored because of the war, as the Rev. Li Tim Oi ministered faithfully to her flock. But at war's end anger exploded. The Archbishop of Canterbury denounced the ordination. Bishop Hall was censured, although he insisted that he only confirmed what the Holy Spirit had ordained. To diffuse the anger directed at Bishop Hall, Li Tim Oi voluntarily gave up her license to function as a priest. Shortly thereafter she was captured by the Communists, placed in a rehabilitation camp, and spent the next 35 years working on a farm and then in a factory. Finally, she obtained a visa to visit her sister in Toronto, Canada. In 1984, forty years to the day after her ordination she was reinstated as a functioning priest in the Anglican Church. She stayed in Toronto and became an Associate at Saint Matthew's parish, where she ministered as a "reluctant celebrity" until her death in 1992.

Many people in the American Church, especially women, note her rejection by the established powers, while they celebrate her devotion, courage and faithfulness. The Rev. Li Tim Oi has almost achieved the status of sainthood.

EFFORT TO OBTAIN CONSENSUS ··

The *Windsor Report* provides examples from recent
history of efforts to obtain consensus before adopting
new policies. The Report used as a positive example the
Bishop of Hong Kong and Macao who in 1968 brought a
new request to the Lambeth Conference asking approval
for the ordination of two women to the priesthood. A
request from Hong Kong prior to 1968 had been placed
on hold with the statement, "The theological arguments
as at present presented for and against the ordination of
women for priesthood are inconclusive." These women
were eventually ordained in 1971 without full support of
the Anglican Communion.

The 1978 Lambeth Conference was confronted
with the reality that without prior agreement Hong
Kong, Canada, the United States, and New Zealand
had all ordained women to the priesthood and eight
other Provinces had accepted ordination in principle.
It was after the fact that the Conference recognized the
right of each Church to make its own decision about the
appropriateness of ordaining women.

The next crisis involved the election and
consecration of women to the office of bishop. The way
this issue was resolved can serve as a model for dealing
with such issues in the future. The Grindrod Report
first counseled restraint in such ordinations, with due
courtesy and respect for those who opposed. It asked
for an extensive dialogue with parties who held different
positions. The Archbishop was asked to encourage and
monitor such dialogue.

Further instruction called for an orderly process if
a Province went ahead with the ordination because of

compelling doctrinal reasons and by strong support from within its Province. Such a step should be recognized and accepted by the world body. The response in Resolution I of the Lambeth meeting of 1988 stated, "That each Province respect the decision and attitudes of other Provinces in the ordination or consecration of women to the episcopate, without such respect necessarily indicating acceptance of the principles involved." Within that context, the Report called for the highest possible degree of communion with the Provinces that differed.

THE CURRENT CONFLICT

Moving now to the current conflict, church leaders in other parts of the world, especially Africa, expressed the view that the Americans were both hasty and haughty in proceeding so quickly with the ordination of the Rev. Canon V. Gene Robinson as bishop of New Hampshire. Archbishop Peter Akinda, Primate of the 18-million member Anglican Church in Nigeria, issued a statement after Convention, "We are astonished that such a high level Convention of the Episcopal Church should conspire to turn their back on the clear teaching of the Bible...The present development compels us to begin to think of the nature of our future relationship."

American church leaders have acknowledged and expressed regret that they failed to bring the matter before the Anglican Consultative Council and ask support and approval for the change in policy. However, since the General Convention of the Episcopal Church meets only once every three years, the timing did not coincide with the perceived urgency of dealing with the issue posed by the Diocese of New Hampshire.

Those of us who are American citizens recognize that to some extent there is a flaw in our psyche brought about by our dominance as a world leader politically and economically. In American foreign policy, we have a tendency to act first and consult only when we want other nations to support our program or if there is strong objection to our action. We wish we had consulted more, but as indicated, we were confronted at that time with this specific issue that we had to address with an up or down vote.

The sense by the African Church that the American church was haughty, some feel, emerges from the long tradition of American missionary work in which the guest missionaries held dominant positions over local church leaders. Others feel that the perception of haughtiness was unavoidable because American money still dictates many mission projects. Perhaps the Church in Africa was reacting in part to past feelings of their perceived subservience and even current resentment in some instances.

To the extent that such feelings have validity, an apology is in order. We, as a Church, are a servant people called to respect the dignity of brothers and sisters in Africa and to work together in mutual trust and care. The writer has spent a great deal of time in Africa and until recently served on an Episcopal-sponsored Foundation working in several countries in Africa. All of us who have worked with the Church in Africa stand in wonder at the depth of commitment and the quality of joy observed among so many Anglican brothers and sisters. We are awed by the evangelistic zeal, which has resulted in winning millions of converts to Christ and the Anglican

Church. We do not always know how to share graciously. While it is more blessed to give than to receive, it is also harder at times to give graciously than to receive in the same spirit.

There is an American side to the story of this break in fellowship. The Episcopal Church has shared its struggle over homosexuality for many years. The worldwide Anglican leadership has been aware of the debates at every General Convention from 1963 to 2003. Further, our Church did invite and pay all of the costs for a large number of bishops from other countries to attend past Conventions and the one in Minneapolis that made this decision. These bishops were invited to hear all sides of the debate. In addition, they were given many opportunities to speak and express their views, which were heard with interest and respect.

A word of witness is in order to the Church in Africa. We note that the Church there has taken a strong emotional stand against homosexuality. We ask the probing question, "why?" This book has noted that the Israelite culture was highly prejudiced toward women, perhaps without realizing it. Women were given in marriage without their consent. They could be divorced by their husbands but had no right of recourse toward their husbands when they were wrongly treated. It was in that context that male homosexuality was forbidden, even condemning a person to death for such practice. Men wanted to be consistent in their domination of women. The act of homosexuality placed one man in the role of a woman, and hence compromised the domination by men.

We have come to believe strongly that God wills equality between men and women. Each is to be respected and treated with equal rights. We acknowledge that this is not always reflected in scripture but it is implicit in the way Jesus accepted all people equally.

We are aware of the inequality of the sexes in much of African society. A recent front-page story in the local newspaper described a community in Kenya where a frightened 13-year-old girl was rescued from an unwanted marriage to a man three times her age.[130] The story describes an all-female village where members help young girls running from forced marriages. It is made up largely of women who were raped and then abandoned by their husbands, who claimed these wives had shamed their community.

The story told how these women have started businesses to support themselves. The next step in the evolution of their agenda is to become politically active. They have a platform for action that is designed to give women the right to refuse marriage proposals, fight sexual harassment in the work place, reject genital mutilation and prosecute rape, an act so frequent that Kenyan leaders call it the nation's greatest human rights issue. Another part of their agenda is to gain specific legal rights if the husband takes a second wife and the first one has reason to fear HIV infection.

We note with appreciation that the Archbishop of Southern Africa, Njongonkuhu Ndungane, recognizes that attitudes of male domination are harmful to women and children and an obstacle to the fight against AIDS. In an interview with *Sojourners* magazine he said, "We need to give loving care and support to people living with AIDS. We're engaged in addressing men, in giving respect and dignity to women. For the past four years I've led an annual men's march in which we say, 'Real men don't abuse women.' We call on men to respect their wives, their sisters, their daughters, and their mothers. One of the joys of these marches is that we see young boys also joining us."[131]

These are the kinds of issues the Episcopal Church in the United States believes are gospel imperatives. They call us to take a stand and witness to justice and fairness as measured by the example and teaching of Jesus. It is in this context that we stand with gay and lesbian persons, believing they were born with predispositions for attraction to persons of the same sex. We believe they should not be excluded or discriminated against because of their God-given sexuality any more than African-Americans should be held in contempt because of their color. This for us is an important issue.

We do recognize strong general cultural differences in attitudes about homosexuality between our country and Africa. The Pew Global Attitudes Project in 2002 studied attitudes toward homosexuality by country. When asked whether homosexuality "should be accepted by society" people in the United States supported acceptance by 69% for and 26% against. The highest percentage in the world opposing homosexuality was in Africa. Uganda and Nigeria reported 95% in opposition and 5% favorable. Kenya had the highest number opposing gays and lesbians in the world, reporting 99% against and 1% favorable. We recognize that our differences have cultural as well as religious roots, much from Islamic sources.

We turn now to issues surrounding homosexuality in England. The Church of England is faced with serious decisions. The way those decisions are made will help determine how much respect the Church has in English society. The United Kingdom, according to the 2002 Pew report, favors accepting homosexuality by 74% in favor to 22% in opposition. The Civil Partnership Act went into effect in December, 2005. It enables same-gender partners to register their relationship with civil authorities and then receive the civil benefits of married couples.

The Church has been divided over its policy when clergymen register. The official response has been to say they can register but in order to continue as clergy in good standing they must take a pledge to remain celibate. A House of Bishops spokesman warned that priests who register will be asked whether their relationship is consistent with the teaching of the Church. But a number of bishops have stated that they do not plan to pry into the sex lives of priests.

The Reverend Richard Kirker, general secretary of the Lesbian and Gay Christian Movement said, "This statement is perfectly consistent with the Church of England's policy of double dealing, duplicity and disregard for decency. It betrays contempt once more for lesbian and gay relationships and should be rejected as unloving, unpastoral and unworkable."[132]

The Church of England's Evangelical Council, representing the traditional position, declared in 1995 that in regard to homosexual persons the Church speaks good news of salvation for all but rejects any claim for acceptance of same-gender relationships. It called such persons to lives of chastity and holiness. It recognized two forms of vocation, marriage and singleness and then concluded, "There is no place for the Church to confer legitimacy upon alternatives to these."

We are vividly aware of how scripture has been misused throughout history. The Bible was used to justify the Crusades with their unspeakable horror against Muslim people. It was used to justify the Roman Catholic Inquisition, the torture and killing of persons who disagreed with official doctrine. The Bible was used to stir anti-Semitism and help justify the Holocaust. It was used to support slavery in the early history of this country and it has been quoted often in support of keeping women in the role of second-class citizens. Indeed, many of the laws in the Old Testament are barbaric by our standards.

This history of abuse of scripture suggests that we must be very careful in using proof-texts to support positions that could be at odds with the gospel of love taught by Jesus. We recognize that this interpretation of scripture may be new to many. We believe that rather than undermine the integrity of God's Word, our view confirms it.

Every major religious group in the United States is dealing with homosexuality. It is an issue that no longer can be avoided either in the church or by government. It is in this context that we feel compelled to face homosexuality, knowing it can no longer be swept under the rug. We recognize that other Provinces are not faced with these pressing claims, nor have they come to the same conclusions.

COOPERATION BUT NOT UNIFORMITY

Our classic Anglican tradition, we feel, provides a way for us to deal with this conflict. The approach was learned from necessity in the 16th and 17th centuries and has served the Church well. At that time Roman Catholicism was unyielding in its belief that it had the corner on divine truth. Protestant reformation groups, especially Geneva Puritans, thought they knew God's will without question. Anglican theology developed in response to these dogmatic opposites. As noted by L. William Countryman, "The one was infallible in principle; the other just behaved as if it were."[133]

Anglicans have preferred to give greater weight to "holy mystery." We are willing to leave many important but contentious issues unanswered at the level beyond core doctrine, recognizing as the Apostle Paul put it, "now we see through a glass darkly." We hold deep convictions about the love of God and the redemption of humanity, but on matters other than core doctrine, we accept differing views among equally sincere people. Since our Church has spoken officially, we also support its decision on homosexuality.

Indeed, the genius of Anglicism is to accept differences and still live together. This Anglican focus on maintaining unity necessarily means a big mansion with many rooms. It houses saints of many descriptions. One way forward is to maintain respect and ongoing dialogue without painting over these differences. The Anglican Communion is a fellowship of Churches. Any effort to make it a world church along Roman Catholic lines is out of character with our tradition. We misconstrue the nature of Anglicism historically if we make this issue a "moment of truth," a fault line with a "shift in tectonic plates" that spells doom for our participation as co-equals in common ministry.

NEW SIGNS OF GRACE

Our critics in the Church accuse us of "going with the flow" of American culture, of being like dead fish, drifting down stream. In fact, our stance, we believe, is the opposite. We stand against prevailing culture in our support of Bishop Robinson, and we choose a road less traveled as compared with the larger fervent evangelical groups in our country and the Roman Catholic Church. They are convinced it is their duty to save us from degradation and spiritual death. It is true that both sides reach conclusions and stand by them. We made our commitment after long and prayerful agony, wanting to do God's will and willing to pay the cost. We cannot surrender our belief that we must respect the dignity of every person. We cannot turn back from understanding that justice for all requires a new attitude on our part. This has not been easy for us. We have had to do much soul-searching before we reached our position. We ask you to hear us prayerfully and see if you can understand, or at least appreciate our position.

We believe that by listening to gay and lesbian persons we have found new insight and signs of grace among us. So we cannot lock the door and close the shutters over the windows. The winds of the Spirit are blowing among us. We recognize that our new position is untidy, disruptive and is spreading dismay among many dear friends. But we understand that we are heralds of a new day in working toward justice for at least five percent of our population. We are opening the door to the kingdom of God for many gay and lesbian persons. So while this action of ours may appear to be untidy, we hail it as a sign. As Jesus suggested, it is like a red sky at night, heralding the dawn of a calm and peaceful morning of justice on some distant day.

The *Windsor Report* notes that there are issues that do not permit acceptance of difference. We cannot say "Some of us are racists; some of us are not, so let's celebrate our diversity." We place rights of gay and lesbian persons in the same category as racial justice, or justice for women. We do not believe this is a matter for compromise or diversity. Yet, we know that many have not joined the struggle. So, despite our strong conviction as to the rightness of our action we still say there is a place for *adiaphora* for things non-essential, as we struggle together to help reform our church and our world.

The *Windsor Report* acknowledges that the Holy Spirit enables the Church to undertake theological developments. The fourth-century creeds go beyond the actual words and concepts of scripture, but they do express the faith of those committed to it. But the report notes that all further development does not carry equal weight. There are heresies as well. Some developments do not enhance the Christian faith but rather distort or even destroy it. We take the position that this development corrects an ancient wrong and positions us in the deep waters of God's ever-flowing grace. We believe this is an important issue; we hope it is not seen as central to the very essence of our faith as Christians. We ask you to struggle with these issues as we are doing.

We note that ten lesbian and gay clergy in the Diocese of Washington responded to the *Windsor Report* with a communication showing appreciation for how The Rt. Rev. John Bryson Chane of their diocese has supported them both publicly and privately. The main point was to note that the Lambeth Commission which produced the report did not include any lesbian or gay persons nor were they asked to testify or respond. "Such a process is contrary to what we understand to be the cornerstone values of Anglican moral and Christian ethics, which require that the voices of those most affected by any decision must be heard."

The Anglican Consultative Council met in Nottingham, England on June 22, 2005 and voted in a first resolution to accept the voluntary withdrawal of the United States and Canadian delegates from official representation. The motion to adopt the resolution came close to failing. A second resolution was passed with almost unanimous consent. It was a call for the Anglican Communion to listen to the experience and perspective of homosexual persons. Leaders of Integrity in the United States and similar organizations in other countries have been called by the Rev. Canon Gregory K. Cameron to come to England and discuss practical ways to open this dialogue.

Where do we go from here? We suggest four paths, all being walked by some, but which together could form a road through the swampland. (1) The American Church can offer sincere apology for failing to communicate and consult more actively during the process of moving toward a change in policy. (2) The Church in each country can study the local conditions in each other's cultures. Each can and should challenge the other but should also exercise tolerance in appreciation of local conditions. For example, the Anglican Communion approved the African practice of polygamous marriage for those already involved prior to their conversion to Christianity. (3) The Episcopal Church USA needs to respond with a biblical and theological rationale as complete as possible, recognizing that this is a legitimate request. (4) All parties will be well served by heeding our traditional stance of maintaining tolerance for difference within a larger unity. We are well advised to dismiss all designs for theological conformity and centralized polity. The Anglican Communion is primarily a fellowship of Churches. It is more than that, but how much more has not been determined.

We would like to share again in the communion of saints and enter together into the joy of our Lord. We trust that we can again restore the old Anglican approach of unity within diversity. We want to do our part.

Chapter 12
CHRIST LOVED THE CHURCH

> After climbing a great hill, one finds many
> more hills to climb.
> —Nelson Mandela as President of South Africa

We step back from the debate over homosexuality and place it in a larger perspective. What is the creative plan of God for the twenty-first century and beyond? What could be the role of the Episcopal Church and other mainline denominations in that plan? How we deal with homosexuality will help to define us both to ourselves and to the national and world communities.

MAINLINE DENOMINATIONS IN FLUX

Mainline denominations in the United States are in an era of flux and transition. These are established church bodies with their buildings dotting the main streets in every village, town and city from the Atlantic to the Pacific oceans. They are struggling to maintain their unity as mansions with many rooms, but now they are pressured to take sides in the culture wars that rage within their sanctuaries and in the public square. Each denomination has always contained "liberals" and "conservatives" but the main thrust of the mainline churches has been "progressive." A new term to characterize them has been suggested by the *Christian Century* magazine as "Christian humanist." We, as Episcopalians, are one of these denominations.

These denominations all recognize the Lordship of Jesus Christ. We believe it is necessary to be "in the world but not of this world." We recognize the world as the good gift of God but know that by human pride, greed, and selfish desire we constantly corrupt what God has given. Therefore, it is our responsibility to discern the injustice in civil life that keeps one race or class or group in subjection. We understand that there are "structural injustices" in the way laws are made and enforced. Therefore, we feel responsible for challenging discrimination, corporate greed, and the power of the rich to buy favors from elected officials. It is our responsibility as Church to evaluate the culture and reject all that is unwholesome, including issues related to human sexuality. And it is our never-ending task to read and understand the Bible in the light of the local, national, and world situation. The mainline denominations have historically been powerful positive witnesses in American society and have supported a political philosophy that served the interests of the poor while seeking fair play and justice for all people. These are the Christian humanists. This is the Episcopal Church in America.

These denominations find their numbers and influence in decline. We are challenged by Christian fundamentalists and their partners on the economic right. We are ignored by secular humanists, people who take our values seriously but who have dropped out of our churches. And we are co-opted by the traditionalists within our ranks. This description holds true for each mainline denomination, but for none is it more accurate than our own.

One room in the Episcopal mansion is inhabited by devout members known as traditionalists. They provide a very different analysis of the problems our denomination faces. For example, a traditionalist, the Reverend John W. Yates II, rector of Falls Church Parish in Falls Church, Virginia, preached a widely distributed sermon to his congregation on July 14, 1996 in which he saw the decline in membership and influence as being caused by denominational leadership falling into modernism or revisionist positions. He stated, "Leadership in the Church. That is really the issue that's before mainline denominations today, not just ours. What sort of people will we ordain in leadership in our churches— theologically, morally, character-wise?" He saw those who want to ordain homosexual persons as revisionists, more Unitarian than Trinitarian, not sure that God should be called "Father." He equated the effort to include homosexual persons as evidence of compromise and weakness, and he indicated that mainline churches put great faith in the culture and often shape their theology to fit current cultural trends. All of this uncertain teaching weakens the church and its ministry, he concluded. In fairness, we note the vigorous, active spirit in that parish, and the recognition by the rector that homosexual persons are children of God who deserve our love and ministry.

CONSERVATIVE OPPONENTS

We have also been attacked from within by individuals with conservative economic positions and by organizations with funding from corporations or individuals with enormous wealth. The attack has been relentless for at least the past fifty years. The current rupture within the Episcopal Church is being fueled by money from such sources just as it is in every other mainline denomination. According to an article in the **Pittsburg Post-Gazette**, the American Anglican Council is leading the charge against the position taken by the Church in General Convention.[134] One of its major sources of funding is Howard F. Ahmanson, Jr. of California, who donates $10,000,000 per year to conservative causes with much of the money flowing to churches or church-related activity. Mr. Ahmanson, an Episcopalian, joined St. James Church in Newport Beach, California, which until recently had as Rector, the Rev. David Anderson, now President of the American Anglican Council. Further research reveals that Mr. Ahmanson inherited more than a half billion dollars at his father's death when he was age 18. Mr. Ahmanson has described himself as being on a mission from God to stop gay marriage, fight evolution and defeat "liberal" churches. He is the major donor to foundations and institutes created to promote "intelligent design." In a magazine article published in 1997 he argued that the Bible opposes minimum wage laws. Finally, for purposes of understanding Mr. Ahmanson, he has identified with a movement to replace the constitution with a fundamentalist theocracy.

The Republican National Committee during the Presidency of Ronald Reagan made a deliberate decision to bring fundamentalist preachers into the White House and link them with conservative economic leaders. During this era the writer was a faculty member at Wesley Theological Seminary in Washington D.C. and taught Political Ethics. Students made regular excursions into the city to study politics and the making of public policy. At the Republican National Committee, we sat in the conference room where, it was explained, Jerry Falwell, Pat Robertson, and other fundamentalist religious leaders had sat. The Roman Catholic priest on the staff explained how in that room they forged an alliance with the administration and the Republican Party. They were to have full access to the White House and the President and their issues would be given prominence, while mainline church leaders would be largely excluded. They would receive financial support from conservative economic leaders. In return, they agreed to organize their constituents to vote Republican. The priest explained how in churches across the country the Sunday worship services were interrupted before the offering so that voter registration forms could be filled out and then collected with the offering.

Millions of persons who had long avoided politics became part of a new religious/political force in American life. This alliance has made strange bedfellows for the past twenty years between ardent "cultural conservative" Christians and country club secularists who see the economic and political advantage. Homosexuality has leaped into the role of a wedge issue to inflame the cultural conservatives and deepen their commitment to the Republican Party.

The aggressive fundamentalist movement has hosted talk shows, radio and television Bible studies, and programs by dozens of preachers who have gathered national followings. To drive across the United States today and listen to the radio is to be bombarded by one fundamentalist program after another. On a recent trip, the writer did not hear a single radio program sponsored by anyone from a mainline church.

At the same time, conservative economic "think-tanks" whose policies are aimed at church audiences have been heavily financed. Their role is to challenge any movement toward economic justice or any new laws that benefit the poor, when they are supported by mainline national church bodies.

THE DEBATE IS JOINED

The Rev. John C. Danforth, Episcopal priest and former Republican senator from Missouri, recently published an opinion editorial in the *New York Times* in which he addressed the culture wars.[135] He noted that the debate is being framed as between people of faith and secular non-believers. He raised his hand to say there is another segment of believers who do not agree with conservative Christians on many important social issues, including homosexuality. Both sides of the religious community are "people of faith," even when they reach differing conclusions. He noted how American politics has become characterized by two phenomena: "the increased activism of the Christian right, especially in the Republican Party, and the collapse of bipartisan collegiality." Senator Danforth suggested there may be a relationship between the two. He rejected the use of wedge issues to create confrontation and division and proposed that humility, tolerance and kindness replace meanness. He made a case for using religion to unite the people of our country, rather than to separate people. Finally the retired Senator, Episcopal priest and recent

Ambassador to the United Nations ended his article with a plea for moderation in the debate over religion and politics.

While mainline churches have maintained much of their humanism, the number of parishioners who share their vision of the kingdom of God as a kingdom of justice, peace and reconciliation has diminished. These churches have largely ignored the fundamentalist movement, while aggressive leaders on the other side have continued to win adherents away from mainline churches and have converted many parishes into conservative outposts.

A common characteristic of fundamentalism is the insistence that the Bible is inerrant. They reason that if any sentence in the Bible is inaccurate or not written by the hand of God, then there is no way to know that anything in the Bible is reliable. They condemn Christians who take a different approach as being "modernists."

Dr. N. T. Wright, a New Testament scholar in the Church of England, considers fundamentalism "a Western modernist game, but the wrong game." It is modern because it was born in America in the nineteenth century. He states his preference for the word "reliable" when applied to scripture. He stated, "I don't like inerrant. That is an Americanism and carries with it a lot of political baggage."[136]

THE SECULARIST MOVEMENT

While fundamentalist churches are growing by leaps and bounds, on the other side, the nation is becoming more secular. Many more educated people no longer strongly identify with the religion faith of

previous generation. A large group inherited high ethical
standards. They carry forward the vision of Christian
humanism but have abandoned the church because to
them it seems irrelevant. When the trumpet sounds its
call to battle for justice, peace and a caring society — all
hallmarks of powerful movements by mainline churches
in the past—we notice that the call now comes from
secular sources, not primarily from the churches.
The bottom line reveals a nation in which mainline
churches, including the Episcopal Church, are in decline.
Many members who attend liturgy regularly are more
influenced by fervent preaching on the radio than by
their own rectors. Social and political issues are being
formulated and forcefully put forward by the religious and
economic right. Then they are countered by the secular
left. But we hear far too little from the perspective of the
mainline churches on important issues of the day.

This dynamic is being played out on the national
stage around the issue of how we treat homosexual
persons in our society and in our churches. Our stand on
this issue affords us an important opportunity to clarify
our identity and make a positive witness to our society
without undue polemics against those who oppose our
position. With prayerful modesty our Church says we
stand firmly for justice toward homosexual persons and
for their acceptance at the highest levels in our Church.
Can this be the authentic Anglican way forward in this
turbulent time?

Europe has gone farther down the path toward
secularism than the United States, in part because
they do not have our populist religious groups. Europe
is predominantly Roman Catholic and the Church

is perceived as out of touch with the real world. It pontificates as if we were in the middle ages, a time long since finished. Europe, for the sake of justice, is not willing to keep women in subordinate roles and exclude them from primary seats at the table. European nations for the sake of justice are passing laws to honor same-gender couples with civil unions, extending to them all civil rights of marriage. If the Church prefers to deny justice, while claiming to be sacred, they prefer the label secular. There are additional causes for European secularism, but clearly the Church is digging its own grave there.

The separation of church and state has become a divisive and dangerous issue in our country. The solid wall of separation is being eroded by those who prefer a theocracy over a neutral government policy. Some question whether there is further cause for alarm with a majority on the Supreme Court being Roman Catholic. A national consensus once held that reference to God could be included in public life but that sectarian appeals should be excluded. As the nation has grown more multi-cultural, with citizens holding religious views different from established Christian assumptions, it has been difficult to maintain the delicate balance. Fundamentalists want to dominate the public square; secularists want to exclude religion as divisive. The two extreme positions contend in the courts and in the media for majority control of popular opinion, while the old mainline consensus evaporates. We need to speak for the right of each religious group to be represented and respected as it openly makes its witness in public places, but do so in ways that respect the right of others to do the same.

Religious witness in public places should be accomplished with civility and due sensitivity to the religious beliefs of the entire community.

TRADITIONALISTS IN THE CHURCH

Within our liturgical Church, which serves as a bridge between Reformation Protestants and ancient Catholics, one of the branches of our tree of faith belongs to the traditionalists. We have previously referred to their analysis of reasons for the decline of our denomination. They find great strength in settled beliefs that have not changed. Their gaze is backward as they seek to be holy by conforming to ancient standards. They are settled in their doctrine, sincere in their beliefs, and shrill in their opposition to change.

Such religious leaders were present in Jesus' day as they are today and are in every age. Jesus gave them low marks. They were the people who worshipped the prophets of the past while condemning the prophets of the present. Jesus put words in their mouths. "If we had lived in the days of our ancestors, we would not have taken part with them in shedding the blood of the prophets. Thus you testify against yourselves that you are descendents of those who murdered the prophets."[137] Jesus proclaimed the message that justice trumps tradition!

Jesus revealed as much about himself on this issue as on any other. Indeed, this issue cost him his life. He openly challenged the Pharisees who lived by rules based on traditional law. Jesus not only drove the money changers out of the temple courtyard but also effectively condemned the whole temple system, long central in the tradition of Judaism. In effect, Jesus made a clean sweep of traditionalism. In its place Jesus equipped his followers by showing them how to use their imaginations to fulfill the law of love. "Once I was blind, but now I can see" described figuratively and literally those touched by the Master.

Traditions are, nonetheless, useful guides. But when times change, new issues arise, and new insights are brought to the forefront, the traditions need to adapt. This is not being "wishy-washy." Traditions stay alive by nourishing a spirit of debate about them. Traditions flourish when they are loved but not loved too much. They should be approached lovingly but also critically.

"Tradition is the living faith of the dead," wrote the Yale religious historian Jaroslav Pelikan. "Traditionalism is the dead faith of the living."

CALL FOR A NEW "HOLINESS CODE"

The Holiness Code found in the middle chapters of Leviticus was an honest effort to define Israel as a holy people, separating their moral character from the Canaanites and surrounding peoples. It represented their desire to stand in the presence of a holy God in wholeness, worthy to be God's chosen people. This code, with its great mixture of noble aspiration and detailed prescriptions of how to act, represented their attempt to define themselves. In Deuteronomy we read the challenge issued by Moses as his last testament before his death, "I have set before you life and death, blessings and curses. Choose life...."[138]

Prophets, walking in the steps of Jesus, are called to speak forth the word of God in each new age and to challenge the traditions with their mixture of good and bad. Self-interest and prejudice that pose as sacred are to be scrutinized and rejected. In that spirit, we as a Church might consider writing a new Holiness Code for our day, taking account of our culture, our global challenges, and the distortions within the religious community that fall short of the ethic of Jesus. Ours then would be a living faith and we would leave to posterity a new noble tradition. What a wonderful challenge for each parish to call forth a group of faithful members of various views to study the life of Jesus, the scriptural context of the original Holiness Code, along with the modern cultural scene and then write their version of a Holiness Code for our day. The collection and coordination of such efforts by the national Church might produce a vital consensus, coming from the grassroots membership. Other denominations might replicate this process within the framework of their own organizations. This project would help reclaim the fundamental values underlying important issues, including the debate over homosexuality. The real question we ask is "What does the Lord require as a holiness code for our day?" To put the question another way, "How can we most fully reclaim Christian fundamentals in the modern world?"

THE GLOBAL RELIGIOUS STRUGGLE

The religious/culture conflict is being waged in every major world religion, along the lines that characterize our own struggle. Our national attention has focused on fundamentalist Islamic groups who wage war against America. They vow to protect their own culture and holy places against western, and especially American, intrusion. Since the subway bombings in

England the novelist and essayist Salman Rushdie has expressed his sense that our nation should do all that is possible to encourage an Islamic reformation. He sees the need to bring the core concepts of Islam into the modern age. New scholars are needed to replace the scriptural literalists and the narrow dogmatism that plagues much present-day Muslim thinking.

Mr. Rushdie believes that Muslim thought must move beyond inerrancy of their scripture so it can be studied as a series of events within history, not supernaturally above it. He believes their holy leaders can revere its message and make it relevant to our times without insisting that it is infallible. Islamic scholars must not allow the fundamentalists to imprison their faith and culture in "iron certainties and unchanging absolutes." Only then can laws made in the seventh century finally give way to the needs of the twenty-first.[139]

The turmoil at the core of our common life in America and around the world is a struggle to find a new consensus, a common vision, as the nations of the world become increasingly interdependent. This is the big story of our day. It is the picture of spaceship earth without borders in which all people recognize that they share a common destiny. There is a rapidly approaching "totalization of the human consciousness." That is to say, people all over the world simultaneously hear the same news, react to the same crises, listen to the same music, and are confronted with the same conflicting ideologies of the world's people.

This realization of our new challenge can release Christians from narrow perspectives and ethnocentric proclamations that God is on our side at the expense of others. For the first time we understand the words from Saint John's gospel, "God so loved the world...." This reality offers the great new agenda for the Church. It is expressed in a new bumper sticker that reads, "God bless the world—all of it."

People who are not at home with these revolutionary changes and are not grounded sufficiently in their own identity naturally recoil in fear and anger at being challenged. Denominations that have not found a way to adjust ancient doctrines to new known scientific truth and social conditions are at a great disadvantage. They fail to understand the tide that is pulling us toward our destiny in God's plan to make the human family truly one. They find strength in elevating values of a by-gone era and a literalist vision of ancient truths.

The biblical vision is the old story that God rules the world. It is the affirmation that God wills all people to live together in fairness, justice, and respect so that all may flourish. God's plan for the ages is taking shape. It is not a sectarian plan that includes a few and rejects everyone else. It is a magnificent plan in which God wills to bring every nation and tribe and people together in a joyous community of humanity. The ancient prophet first proclaimed the vision, "The earth shall be full of the knowledge of the Lord as the waters cover the seas."[140]

When we affirm with the writer of Revelation that "Christ shall put all things under his feet" we believe he is stamping out small thinking, discrimination, partisan advantage, self-centered power struggles and the rich taking advantage of the poor. He is calling us to world community because he is the God of all humanity.

The inability of some parts of our religious and secular community to come to grips with this new world causes them to pull back into cultural or theological isolation. It makes people want to protect what is theirs at the expense of others. Many of us fight back blindly against the seeming encroachment of other faiths and cultures.

This is the real struggle going on in the world. It is reflected in the makeup of every major world religion. There are the "fundamentalists" forces in every religion pulling back and rejecting the new world. They may call for a "jihad," killing the infidels in movements such as those led by Osama bin Laden. But in Islam, Hinduism, Buddhism, Judaism, and Christianity there are also those who are reaching out to embrace what we hold in common. We believe that our day calls the Church to affirm the building of a world safe for diversity. We believe it is possible to affirm the essentials of our own faith without excluding or depreciating the search for God in the traditions of others.

As Episcopalians, our hope for the future envisions a collegial and cooperative relationship with the Primates and Provinces of the worldwide Anglican Communion. We pray each Lord's Day for "Rowan our Archbishop" that he will be guided in leading wisely this dedicated but disparate collection of national churches. We recognize that unity within our own household that tolerates differences is our foremost and best witness to a larger global unity of all Christians. We are compelled by the prayer of our Lord in John's gospel to always search for that unity, "that they may be one."[141]

As we seek a larger Christian unity within the diversity of Church and sect, at another level we reach out to people of all religions. We do not compromise our basic beliefs, our creeds or our ancient affirmations. Nonetheless, we walk together in love with those of all races and religions, sharing our beliefs with them while being open to learn from them.

Christians, along with serious seekers in all religions, are not being called to a second-class sideshow. Rather, we are invited to participate in the main event of history. Indeed, we are invited to make history, to reveal through our tradition the love offered by Jesus, and to proclaim the vision of God's rule over the world. The affirmation of personhood and justice for homosexual persons is one piece in the great mosaic that is forming as the world moves to higher standards of human rights in God's grand design for an entire humanity worthy of providing hospitality to the Almighty.

AN INSPIRED VISION

This vision requires the Episcopal Church to join hands with other denominations to educate great theologians, produce keen Christian ethicists, challenge our priests and pastors to inspired ministry, and expect our communicants to rise to the occasion. We all share in the challenge as together we stake out an unapologetic mission of preaching the gospel of justice, love, and service. We rejoice as we discern signs of the kingdom breaking through around us. We evangelize as we serve. We accept our role as being the light of the world, the beacon set on the hill. We do not imply in any way that we are alone in service to Christ. We reach out to all who call him "Lord."

This is the Church universal that Christ loved and gave himself for!

ENDNOTES

Chapter 1. Wrestling with God

[1] Christian Century, December 13, 2005.
[2] *Washington Post*, December 2, 2005.

Chapter 2. An Affirmation of Inclusion

[3] Doughtonu, Sandi; *Seattle Times*, June 19, 2005.
[4] James Clark & Co.; Cambridge, England; 1991.
[5] For further information and current happenings, go to the web-site for Integrity, www.IntegrityUSA.org.

Chapter 3. A Pastoral Perspective

[6] Institute for Servant Leadership; Vol. 15, No.3, May-June, 1998.
[7] *Robert C. Byrd: Child of the Appalachian Coal Fields*, Robert C. Byrd; West Virginia University Press; Morgantown, June 2005.
[8] *Chicago Tribune*; February 15, 2005.
[9] *Christian Century*; March 8, 2005.
[10] Edited by Beth Ann Gaede.

Chapter 4. Justice Transcends Tradition

[11] Matthew 23:24.
[12] *Washington Post*, March 5, 2005.
[13] *Washington Post*, March 28, 2005.
[14] Bailey, J. Michael, *The Man Who Would Be Queen:*

The Science of Gender-Bending and Transsexualism, Joseph Henry Press, 2003.

[15] Tanis, Rev. Dr. Justin, *Transgendered: Theology, Ministry and Communities of Faith*, Pilgrim Press, 2003.

[16] *New Yorker*, August 1, 2005, by Jeffrey Toobin.

[17] *Washington Post*, May 25, 2005.

[18] *Washington Post*, July 18, 2005.

Chapter 5. The Witness of Scripture

[19] Genesis 19:8.

[20] Genesis 19:14.

[21] Judges 19:22.

[22] Judges 19:25.

[23] Leviticus 18:22.

[24] Leviticus 20:13.

[25] *Virginia Seminary Journal* – Winter, 1996-1997.

[26] Leviticus 18:1-5.

[27] Leviticus 18:20.

[28] Leviticus 19:19.

[29] Deuteronomy 22:5.

[30] Deuteronomy 21:18.

[31] Deuteronomy 21:10-14.

[32] Leviticus 19:18.

[33] Isaiah 1:10, 3:9; Jeremiah 23:14; Ezekiel 16:49-50.

[34] Luke 10:10-12; Matthew 10:5-15.

[35] Luke 17:18-30; Matthew 11:24.

[36] Matthew 8:5-13.

[37] Temple, Gary, "The Biblical Case in Favor of Gene Robinson's Election, Confirmation and Consecration."

[38] Romans 2:1.

[39] Romans 3:23.

[40] Romans 3:26.

[41] Romans 1:26-27.

[42] Canton, Christopher L. and Thompson, Pauline A., Editors, *An Honorable Estate: Marriage, Same-Sex Unions and the Church*, Anglican Book Centre, Toronto, Canada, 1998.

[43] I Corinthians 5:9.

[44] I Corinthians 6:11.

[45] I Corinthians 5:13.

[46] The writer has studied the biblical analysis of homosexuality in several official documents issued by denominations as well as the work of individual scholars within the Episcopal Church. Perhaps Arland J. Hultgren and Walter F.Taylor for the Evangelical Lutheran Church in America wrote the best-balanced account. Their work is titled, *Background Essays on Biblical Texts* and is part of the denomination's study materials titled, "Journey Together Faithfully, Part Two: The Church and Homosexuality," September 2003.

Chapter 6. Law, Wisdom, and the Love Ethic of Jesus

[47] Luke 4:31.

[48] Luke 6:1-11.

[49] Luke 11:37-40.

[50] Matthew 5:17-20.

[51] Luke 10:27.

[52] Matthew 23:23-24.

[53] *Strenuous Commands: The Ethic of Jesus*, A.E.

Harvey, SCM Press, 1990. This Chapter relies heavily on his scholarship.

[54] Proverbs 12:8.

[55] Proverbs 14:21.

[56] Proverbs 14:31.

[57] Proverbs 19:17.

[58] Proverbs 10:12.

[59] Proverbs 19:11.

[60] Matthew 5:39.

[61] Proverbs 15:17.

[62] Luke 6:42.

[63] Proverbs 12:16.

[64] Matthew 7:24-28.

[65] Psalm 1:1; Psalm 127:5; Proverbs 3:13.

[66] Matthew 5:27-28.

[67] Matthew 5:29-30.

[68] Matthew 5:31-32.

[69] Leviticus 20:10.

[70] Proverbs 6:32.

[71] Proverbs 19:14.

[72] Proverbs 19:13.

[73] Matthew 5:43-48.

[74] Deuteronomy 7:1-2.

[75] Psalm 137:7-9.

[76] Exodus 23:4.

[77] Proverbs 27:14.

[78] Luke 6:27-28.

[79] Luke 23:34.

[80] Matthew 5:45.

[81] Luke 6:35.

[82] Luke 20:47.

[83] Leviticus 19:2.

[84] Matthew 5:48.
[85] Luke 10:25-29.
[86] Luke 10:37.
[87] Luke 6: 37-38.

Chapter 7. Right and Good in Christian Ethics

[88] Gibran, Kahil; *Sand and Foam*, Alfred A. Knopf; New York, 1975, p. 36.
[89] Niebuhr, Richard; *The Responsible Self*; New York: Harper and Row, 1963, p. 55.

Chapter 8. The Ways of God: A Theological Perspective

[90] Exodus 3:1-12.
[91] Written in preparation for the General Convention of 2003 in Minneapolis.
[92] Genesis 2: 16.
[93] Genesis 3:18.
[94] Genesis 9:3.
[95] Genesis 9:4-5.
[96] Acts15:15-20.
[97] Calvin, John, *Institutes* IV.10.20.
[98] *Book of Common Prayer*, Articles of Religion, 1801, Number XIX, p. 871.
[99] Numbers 27:1-11.
[100] *Book of Common Prayer*, Articles of Religion of 1801, Article IX, "Of Original or Birth-Sin," page 869.
[101] Mark 1:15.
[102] Matthew 11:29-30.
[103] Romans 3:23.

Chapter 9. Christian Words from Homosexual Persons

[104] Laumann, Gagnon, Michael and Michaels, 1994.

[105] The General Social Survey of 1995.

[106] The story of the AIDS quilts and the marches is recorded in the book, *Love Undetectable* by Andrew Sullivan, (Alfred A. Knoff, New York, 1999) an Episcopal layperson in the Diocese of Washington and then Editor of the New Republic magazine. This writer shared the quilt experience as a member of Saint Augustine's Episcopal Church in southwest Washington, D.C. He experienced and observed this remarkable outpouring of grief and hope and he marched with gay and lesbian members of his congregation, as well as others who supported the cause.

Chapter 10. A Case for Same-Gender Marriage

[107] Genesis 26:14.

[108] Genesis 30:1-13.

[109] Genesis 28:9.

[110] Exodus 20:17.

[111] I Samuel 25:42, 43.

[112] I Kings 10:8.

[113] I Kings 11:3.

[114] Genesis 29: 22.

[115] Judges 14:8-12.

[116] Ezekiel 16:8.

[117] Genesis 24:60, Ruth 4:11-12.

[118] Psalm 19:5, Joel 2:16.

[119] Deuteronomy 24:5.

[120] Mark 10:9.

[121] Mark 10:7-8.

[122] I Corinthians 7:7.

[123] *Book of Common Prayer*, p. 425.

[124] *Washington Post*, January 20, 2005.

[125] *New York Times*, March 31, 2005.

[126] Perrin, Ellen C., "Technical Report: Co-parent or Second-Parent Adoption by Same-Sex Parents," *Pediatrics*, February, 2002.

[127] Ellison, Marvin M., *Same-Sex Marriage? A Christian Ethical Analysis*, The Pilgrim Press, Cleveland, 2004. This book has provided valued insights and perspectives on same-gender marriage.

Chapter 11. Letter to the Anglican Communion

[128] The Lambeth Commission on Communication: *Windsor Report* 2004, Page 13; The Anglican Communion Office, London, UK.

[129] *Washington Post*, April 2, 2005.

[130] *Washington Post*, July 9, 2005.

[131] *Sojourners*, July, 2005.

[132] Bates, Stephen; *The Guardian*, July 26, 2005.

[133] Countryman, L. William; "Dealing with Conflict as Anglicans," *Witness* magazine, General Convention 2003 Edition. This article appeared as a position paper immediately prior to the 74th General Convention. Dr. Countryman is Sherman E. Johnson Professor of Biblical Studies at the Church Divinity School of the Pacific; Berkeley, California.

Chapter 12. Christ Loved the Church

[134] *Pittsburg Post-Gazette*, Sept. 26, 2003.

[135] *New York Times*, June 17, 2005.

[136] Libby, Bob, "Biblical Scholar N.T. Wright Defends Scripture's Reliability," *The Living Church*, June 9, 1996.

[137] Matthew 23: 30-31.

[138] Deuteronomy 30:19.

[139] "The Right Time for an Islamic Reformation," *Washington Post,* August 7, 2005.

[140] Isaiah 11:9.

[141] John 17:11.

APPENDIX
Background Information About the Episcopal Church

The history of the Episcopal Church began with the English exploration and colonization of North America. New England colonies were established by Puritans who opposed Anglicanism. Yet large numbers of Anglicans settled in the southern colonies and the Church of England became the established church in the Carolinas, Maryland, and Virginia.

The Episcopal Church suffered badly during the American Revolution. Loyalties of lay persons and priests split between supporting the British Crown or declaring for the colonists. It was hard to be a fence-sitter. People had to choose. The "established" church had never been popular in the colonies and non-members resented paying taxes to provide financial support to the Anglican Church.

Established Church growth had also been hindered during the colonial period by the absence of a bishop, whose presence was required to ordain priests and conduct confirmations. Britain's colonies were assigned to the Diocese of London, but no bishop ever visited in the new world, isolating Americans from the mother church.

Following the American Revolution, a group of Anglican clergy in Connecticut elected Samuel Seabury, a former missionary in New York, to be their bishop. He was dispatched to England for consecration but the bishop of London denied the request from Connecticut because Seabury would not swear an oath of loyalty to the British Monarch. Seabury traveled on to Scotland where in 1784 he was consecrated by three Scot bishops of the "disestablished" Anglican Church. The English Church soon reconsidered its position and in 1786 consecrated William White of Pennsylvania and Samuel Provoost of New York.

Lay and clergy from several colonies met in Philadelphia in 1789, constituted themselves as deputies, adopted a constitution and revised the Book of Common Prayer. They decided to meet every three years as a General Convention. Governance of their newly founded Church was influenced strongly by the democratic experiment in this country. Clergy and laity comprise the senior house, while the junior house belongs to the bishops. The House of Deputies has always retained the authority to override any action of the bishops.

Each geographical area was designated as a diocese. Elected representatives of parishes, clergy and laity, elect their diocesan bishops, who must then be approved by a majority of Diocesans and diocesan Standing Committees of the entire Church, again elected by representatives of diocesan parishes. This democratic arrangement differs greatly from that in most parts of the Anglican Communion.

Following the American Revolution, England sent colonial bishops across the world to minister to English persons living in the colonies, but they also reached out to do missionary work among the indigenous natives, thereby facilitating the development of the Anglican Communion. American churchmen sent missionaries across the continent of North America and overseas. Hence, the official name: Domestic and Foreign Missionary Society of the Protestant Episcopal Church in the United States of America. Today dioceses participating in General Convention include the countries of Central America, Haiti, the US Virgin Islands, the Dominican Republic, Ecuador and Venezuela.

The American Church accepted the three part nature of Anglican theology: the importance of scripture, tradition and reason. Grappling with scripture became central to the church here. Tradition was honored by accepting the historic episcopate as continuing the true apostolic succession. Reason brought scientific truth and changing experience into focus, requiring new grappling with scripture.

In 1867 at the urging of the Anglican Church in Canada the Archbishop of Canterbury invited the leader of the Church in each country, known as a Primate, to come to England for a conference. The group met at Lambeth and regular meetings become known as The Lambeth Conference. The term "Anglican Communion" described the reality that there was no legislative structure or enforcement power but rather Anglicans were in communion with each other. In 1878 it was agreed that these conferences would be held every ten years and that resolutions would be advisory only. They were always led by the Archbishop of Canterbury, appointed by the British Monarch, and recognized as primus inter pares, or "first among equals."

The dissolution of the British Empire brought greater autonomy for the national churches and helped generate the impetus for more consultation. Between

1979 and 1997 the 38 Primates of their autonomous national churches began to meet every two or three years, and since the year 2000, each year.

The Anglican Consultative Council was formed as a result of a resolution at the 1968 Lambeth Conference. All member Churches accepted its constitution and the Council came into being in October of 1969. Meeting every three years or so, the Council was designed to provide more frequent and representative contact among the churches. Its express role has been to facilitate cooperation, exchange information, and coordinate common action. Membership is comprises of one to three persons from each province. If three, there is one bishop, a priest and a lay person. Where fewer are eligible, lay persons are preferred over bishops. This body has a permanent London-based Secretariat, which also supports the Lambeth Conferences and the Primate Meetings.

In 2003, after the Episcopal Church General Convention, the Primates requested The Lambeth Commission to address the election and consecration of Bishop Gene Robinson and the Canadian Diocese of New Westminster's adoption of rites to bless same sex unions. It also agreed to address the interference by some bishops into other bishops' jurisdictions, as when an African bishop claimed jurisdiction over a dissident congregation and priest within the Diocese of Virginia.

The Lambeth Commission on Communion published its report (Windsor Report) at a news conference in St. Paul's Cathedral, London, on Monday, October 18, 2004.

HORSERADISH

When I was broke and hopeless
Bob called with good work editing
a book he'd written on the Gay Bishop,
a controversial topic, and religion
with little hope of being published.
We worked hard but broke often
to discuss issues and eat ham sandwiches with horseradish.
He said horseradish saved his cousins during the Depression –
they sold it homemade from a horsedrawn wagon.
We looked out the window
and he explained Hollin Hills architecture –
Sometimes he went swimming
and I went back to work in a house with vacuumed carpets
and sat behind a brand new computer with the manuscript.
Forget the arguments.
Bob had seen 80 years of ideas, and their consequences
from penicillin to incendiary bombing.
He'd listened to medieval sermons and Harvard Marxists.
He'd seen ideas strangle one another for preeminence
or suicide without reason.
And he'd known visions to stay on the horizon
yet their light still led him
and the one now he held high in hopes
of changing minds and saving lives,
he would drop to talk about horseradish.

Sidney "Pepper" Smith